What people are saying about …

ONE CHOICE *Away from* CHANGE

"When I think of leaders who have done the work to lead from a place of true health, healing, and hope, I think of Justin and Trish Davis. Their resilience hasn't come easy. But when they write about breaking cycles, they do so from a deeply personal place that comes out in pastoral hearts. I love and respect them immensely."

Lisa Whittle, bestselling author, Bible teacher, host of *Jesus Over Everything* podcast

"Change isn't just about wanting something different—it's about the courage to make the hard, necessary choice to have something different. I admire Justin and Trisha's transparency and believe this book will offer hope to so many who are ready to pursue healing and transformation."

Jon Acuff, bestselling author of *Soundtracks, the Surprising Solution to Overthinking*

"Justin and Trisha courageously share their journey of breaking free from the damaging cycles that once held them captive. Their story is a powerful reminder that true transformation isn't just about wanting change—it's about making the intentional choices that lead to lasting change. This book is for anyone desiring something different."

Rory Vaden, cofounder of Brand Builders Group, *New York Times* bestselling author of *Take the Stairs*

"I am thankful Justin and Trisha have allowed their experiences to further the kingdom of God. Their vulnerability, honesty, and transparency give us the blueprint to make real change. It won't be easy and can be painful, but Justin and Trisha have shown us it is possible. So let's follow their lead and bring joy to the Lord and to our relationships."

Justin Holiday, thirteen-year NBA veteran, world champion with the 2015 Golden State Warriors

"In *One Choice Away from Change*, Justin and Trisha hold nothing back. They share their hurts, haunts, and heartache in a vulnerable yet restorative way that provides hope and redemption for both the young believer as well as the wayward, heartbroken follower of Christ who simply needs that faithful reminder—you are never too far gone."

Christa Hardin, MA, author, therapist, podcast host

"I am the product of these words. Literally, the life I'm now living is—in large part—due to the painstaking work my parents undertook to unwind layers upon layers of generational sin. Let their brilliant storytelling and sober honesty in the pages ahead stir within you a desire to choose change."

Micah E. Davis, pastor of Teaching & Vision at The Sanctuary, author of *Trailblazers*

"Justin and Trish give us the gift of courage to take a look at our hearts and start to make practical, healthy changes toward thriving connections. No gimmicks, no shame; just a whole lot of encouragement cheering us on toward being our best selves so those we know and love can experience the best 'us' possible."

Dave Dummitt, senior pastor of
Willow Creek Community Church

"We're all broken in some way or another, and sadly, many of us let that brokenness affect the relationships we value most. I respect Justin and Trisha so much for having the courage to share their story, and I know it'll help so many others turn the page to pursue health and wholeness."

Adam Weber, lead pastor of Embrace
Church, author, podcaster

"Unfortunately, pain is the common language of humanity, but God wants us to be fluent in the language of heaven and healing. Justin and Trish have created a practical tool that will help you build a better life. A life marked by freedom where you can take a deep breath and continue to distance yourself from the cycles of dysfunction."

Jon Weece, Southland Christian Church

"I often tell my clients if they want to regain power in their lives, we must get to the root and break the dysfunctional cycles that hold them back. In *One Choice Away from Change*, Justin and Trisha Davis provide a step-by-step guide to understanding and breaking free from dysfunctional cycles to lay hold of the life God has in store for you."

Rachael Gilbert, MA MFT, LPC,
author of *Image Restored*, podcast
host, owner of BBC Health

"Every one of us has inherited generational behaviors and choices that we'd rather not repeat. But Justin and Trish provide the encouragement and resources we all need to break our painful cycles and the lies we have believed. If you're looking for lasting transformation in your life and relationships, this book is exactly the toolkit you need."

Kristen Hallinan, author of *Legacy Changer*, host of the *Up Until Now* podcast

"No relationship is perfect, but God uses imperfect relationships to perfect us. As we embrace the growth God invites us to and make different choices, we find freedom and growth. We've experienced the truths on these pages in our own lives. Thank you, Justin and Trisha, for providing a clear road map to change."

Mark and Jill Savage, authors of *No More Perfect Marriages*

"Justin and Trisha have crafted a heartfelt guide for anyone struggling with destructive patterns and cycles. Rooted in biblical wisdom and vulnerability, this book invites readers to find truth and freedom in a journey of faith, healing, and hope."

Jason VanRuler, psychotherapist and author of *Get Past Your Past*

"Justin and Trisha's honesty and willingness to share the difficult things in life allow the reader to see better what hope looks like, and more importantly, that they are not alone. This is a must-read. I do not doubt that anyone reading this will see themselves written on the pages in the most beautiful and restorative way, that beauty can rise out of the ashes."

Jenni Wong Clayville, pastor, speaker

"We all want to break through when we feel stuck, but achieving it means identifying and dealing with the choices and behaviors that got us where we are. This book is a powerful account of broken cycles and restored relationships. Most of all, it is a reminder that it is never too late to find hope and healing."

Josh Surratt, lead pastor of Seacoast Church

"Justin and Trish Davis are the real deal. They are passionate about helping people find freedom, and they know firsthand that in order to get free you have to recognize your patterns that are holding you captive. This book will help you do just that. I highly recommend *One Choice Away from Change.*"

Jackie Brewster, certified Enneagram
coach, author, and speaker

"A couple of years ago, I had dinner with Justin and Trish. At some point, we all cried at that Chinese restaurant that night. But even then, despite the pain, I could see they were on a path toward healing. It inspired me in my own journey of healing, and I know what has now become a book will help you in your healing journey as well."

Jeff Henderson, author of *What to Do Next*

"Justin and Trisha have masterfully woven bits of their own personal experiences with paradigm-shifting insight on how to break the cycles that bog us down and keep us from living a life of wholeness. This is a must-read for anyone wanting to be the best version of themselves."

Davey Blackburn, author of *Nothing is Wasted*, host of the *Nothing is Wasted Podcast*, founder of Nothing is Wasted Ministries

"This book is a lifeline and toolbox for people caught in toxic fight cycles, unsure how to find their way out. Justin and Trisha's raw vulnerability about their own struggles and breakthroughs will bring hope and clarity to anyone feeling stuck. Their honesty inspires the courage for others to break free of shame and move toward true connection."

Casey Caston, founder and CEO of Marriage365

"Justin and Trisha remind us that it's not enough to just want change, we have to be willing to make the hard choices that lead to it. This book is a road map for anyone wanting to break free from the falsehoods that keep us from experiencing true freedom and new beginnings."

Aaron Brockett, lead pastor of Traders Point Christian Church

"We sing of God's favor being upon our family, our children, and their children for a thousand generations. But families can pass on dysfunction, hurt, shame, and brokenness, until one generation makes the courageous choice to change. Justin and Trisha have given us a game-changing gift of help and hope to the future generations of every family."

Gene Appel, senior pastor of Eastside Christian Church, Anaheim, CA

JUSTIN *and* TRISHA DAVIS

ONE CHOICE

Away from

CHANGE

*Break the Cycles That
Hurt Your Relationships
and Hold You Back*

DAVID C COOK

transforming lives together

We dedicate this book to our children and the future generations of our family. May the love you have for God be grounded in the choices we made to change the trajectory of your story.

ONE CHOICE AWAY FROM CHANGE
Published by David C Cook
4050 Lee Vance Drive
Colorado Springs, CO 80918 U.S.A.

Integrity Music Limited, a Division of David C Cook
Brighton, East Sussex BN1 2RE, England

DAVID C COOK®, the graphic circle C logo and related marks
are registered trademarks of David C Cook.

The website addresses recommended throughout this book are offered as a
resource to you. These websites are not intended in any way to be or imply an
endorsement on the part of David C Cook, nor do we vouch for their content.

Library of Congress Control Number 2024951468
ISBN 978-0-8307-8575-9
eISBN 978-0-8307-8576-6

The Team: Michael Covington, Kevin Scott, James Hershberger,
Brian Mellema, Michael Fedison, Jack Campbell, Karen Sherry
Cover Design: Micah Kandros
Cover Author Bio Photo: Olivia Doerfler Photography

Printed in the United States of America
First Edition 2025

1 2 3 4 5 6 7 8 9 10

121624

CONTENTS

FOREWORD

One Choice Away from Change is a powerful, life-changing guide that invites readers to step into a new season of healing, growth, and transformation. With grace and wisdom, this book helps you identify the destructive cycles that have held you back and kept you stuck in unhealthy patterns, whether in relationships or within yourself.

What makes this book so unique is its emphasis on the one choice —that crucial, liberating decision that can break the cycle of dysfunction and propel you toward true freedom. Justin and Trish offer a compassionate approach that guides you through the process of healing, acknowledging the necessary and often painful journey of grief that leads to lasting change. But perhaps most importantly, this book encourages you to let go of the illusion of control and trust God, finding peace in the surrender that allows true transformation to take root.

For anyone feeling weighed down by decision fatigue, *One Choice Away from Change* offers clarity. It's a reminder that healing doesn't require endless choices or perfect steps—it begins with one brave decision to step forward in faith and embrace the possibility of change. If you're ready to break free from cycles that hurt your relationships and limit your potential, this book is for you. It's a profound invitation to heal, grow, and discover the freedom that comes when you trust God to guide you toward a new way of living.

Jarrett and Jeanne Stevens, lead pastors of
Soul City Church, bestselling authors of *Praying
Through* (Jarrett) and *What's Here Now?* (Jeanne)

INTRODUCTION

Trisha and Justin Davis

We grew up in the iconic 1980s, where boys wore tube socks up to their knees and shorts that barely covered their thighs. Girls wore bedazzled sweaters and T-shirts that hung off one shoulder. Eighties hairstyles required so much hair product that we may have unknowingly triggered climate change. Seat belt laws didn't take effect until the late '80s, so road trips meant hanging out the window to high-five the people in the car next to you. The internet was invented in 1983, but it took a whole decade for the public to gain access. We didn't know what we didn't know.

What I (Trisha) loved most about the '80s was school. I grew up in Joliet, Illinois, and attended Forest Park Elementary, where the students and staff were of diverse ethnicities and backgrounds. The curriculum was a pilot program called Individualized Education in which students were given "pass/fail" marks instead of letter grades. We had standard classes in the morning and creative arts in the afternoon. There, I learned how to line dance, make poetry, read music, and navigate a floppy disk.

We called our teachers by their first names—which will take those of you who grew up in the South a minute to wrap your mind around, but being on a first-name basis with my teachers was all I knew. My homeroom teacher, Vanessa, introduced our class to Whitney Houston and Michael Jackson on vinyl. She cried with us as we watched the space shuttle *Challenger* explode live on TV. She was our best friend because, after all, we were on a first-name basis.

One morning, I discovered the most beautiful little "purses" underneath my mom's bathroom sink. They were square, violet with white flowers, and the size of my little hand—the perfect size to hold a Polly Pocket or Barbie accessories. There was a whole box of them, which, to me, meant I could share them with friends at school. When I got to school, I placed a beautiful purse—violet with white flowers—on all the girls' desks, but before I could finish, my bestie, Vanessa, asked me to come with her to the hallway.

I thought I must have hurt Vanessa's feelings by not placing a purse on her desk, but once we got to the hallway, she knelt on one knee and asked where I'd found my gifts. I told her my story, and straight-faced, she explained that the "purses" were not meant for Polly Pockets but for maxi pads. Unable to hold back her giggles,

Vanessa said I couldn't hand them out. I cried hard tears that morning because I didn't know what maxi pads were or why it mattered. How could she not see them for a different use? But she was the adult, and I was the kid, and adults always knew best. I didn't know what I didn't know.

You may have never gifted your elementary school classmates maxi pads, but you probably have your own stories of not knowing what you didn't know.

One afternoon a few months ago, Trish mentioned to me (Justin) that the garbage disposal wasn't working. After acknowledging her concern, I asked if she had tried the reset button on the bottom of the disposal. She said she hadn't, but acknowledged that could be the problem. Even after twenty-five-plus years of marriage, I somehow assumed my job was done.

A couple of days later, while I was rinsing a dish, water started backing up in the sink. Worse was the smell coming from what seemed like the depths of a rotten food pit. I covered my face so as not to gag and flipped the switch to turn on the garbage disposal. Nothing happened but the sound of a hum coming from under the sink.

I turned to Trish and said, "What is going on with this horrendous smell in the sink?"

She said, "I told you two days ago that the garbage disposal wasn't working. Water is backing up because there is food in the drain."

I may be the least mechanical person alive, but opening the doors under the sink, I thought, *If I pretend I know what I'm doing, maybe I'll somehow figure out what to do.* I remembered the reset button I had said would solve the problem and pushed the button, expecting a quick fix. Nothing changed. Still just a hum.

Not wanting to appear weak or ill-equipped, I lay down inside the kitchen cabinet and texted a friend who is mechanically inclined: "Hey bro, what brand of garbage disposal do you recommend? Mine is only two years old, and it's not working."

The brand of garbage disposal he suggested was the same one I was staring at under my sink. I said, "That's what I have, but it's not working." Then he called me.

"Do you have power?"

"Yes, I have power."

"Does it hum?"

"Yes."

"Have you used the Allen wrench on it yet?"

What Allen wrench was he speaking of? I had no clue, but I said, "I was just getting ready to do that. Thanks, man."

I hung up the phone, and still under the sink, I pulled up YouTube and searched, "How to use an Allen wrench on a garbage disposal." Following directions, I felt around the back of the disposal and found an Allen wrench labeled "Garbage Disposal Tool." Grabbing that wrench like a professional plumber, I put it in the slot on the bottom of the disposal and gave it a few turns. Something snapped and released.

I didn't know what I didn't know—until I did, and it changed everything!

Sometimes, not knowing something leads to innocent mistakes, like bringing "purses" to school and passing them out to classmates. But when we gain knowledge and maturity, it can change our perspective and use of what we don't understand.

Other times, our indifference to what we don't know can cause problems that could have been addressed earlier and easier if we had only engaged and learned how to move forward. The problems, issues, and brokenness we live with continue to bring a stench into our human relationships and our relationship with God.

Do you ever wonder why you have difficulty finding and maintaining healthy relationships? Or why, no matter how hard you try, you still lose your temper with those you love the most? Have you experienced the same financial problems year after year, regardless of how much money you make? Do you repeat the same mistakes even though you know the consequences?

What is the solution? Do you simply need to try harder? Do you need to be more disciplined?

The information we share in this book is deeply personal. The choices we outline are principles we've learned and cycles in our marriage and family that we had to identify and break.

Most of us don't change until the pain of staying the same is greater than the pain of change. That certainly was true for us in 2005.

Three years after planting our first church, Justin had an affair with Trisha's best friend. Our ministry was over, and our marriage was on life support. We separated for two months—didn't even talk for ten days—and had a mediator help get our kids back and forth between us. Our future as a family was bleak. We didn't know it yet, but the restoration we needed required our willingness to see beyond the immediate circumstances and pain of the affair and address the cycles of dysfunction woven into the fabric of our marriage and family.

We spent four years of hard work engaging in counseling, self-reflection, truth telling, forgiveness, and creating a new and authentic marriage. In 2009, we were restored to ministry. Justin was hired as a campus pastor at Cross Point Church in Nashville, Tennessee, and we started sharing our story to help others have an extraordinary marriage. We wrote a book and traveled nationwide, investing in marriages. We started a church, did pastoral counseling, coached couples, and hosted marriage retreats. We thought the difficult work of breaking cycles was complete.

Then, in 2021, truth bombs went off in our extended families—unearthing family secrets, lies, manipulation, and generational cycles of brokenness—that shook the foundation of our family, our faith, and everything we thought was true. Once again, we found ourselves in a place of brokenness and devastation. We needed deep healing to avoid passing the pain along to our kids. We knew these destructive cycles had to end with us.

Over the last four years, we've done deep work—individually and as a couple—to identify, excavate, and heal repetitive mindsets, choices, and cycles in our marriage and family. As marriage coaches, we've worked with hundreds of couples who bring cyclical issues into our office looking for a road map to change and transformation. We have learned a universal truth for every relationship: what isn't healed is often repeated. We repeat cycles of behavior in all aspects of our lives that bring hurt, disappointment, discouragement, and exhaustion.

Proverbs speaks to our instinct to repeat choices that aren't wise: "As a dog returns to its vomit, so a fool repeats his foolishness" (26:11).

Most often, we don't struggle with new sins; we struggle with the same sins over and over again. We don't disagree over new issues in our relationships; we argue over the same problems over and over again. When faced with issues at work, we can change jobs, but we often experience the same difficulty in our new jobs. You can likely look back at failed dating relationships or a former marriage and see a pattern of behavior that ended those relationships. Hard as it can be to come to grips with the truth, in all your destructive choices, the common denominator is you.

If you are feeling stuck in a relationship, if you are feeling hopeless that anything will change in your relationships, if you believe that you will never become the person God is calling you to be, this book is for you.

There is so much at stake in finding freedom from these repeated cycles. Your struggles and repeated choices didn't start with you, and unless addressed, won't end with you. What you've inherited doesn't have to be passed on, and what you've chosen in the past out of habit, heartbreak, or hurt doesn't have to define who you become in the future.

How can we break the cycles that leave us wounded and broken? How can we break free from choices that bring hurt and make new choices that bring healing?

Change is possible. Restoration is available. A new beginning can be one choice away.

This book is not an antidote but more of a road map to breaking the cycles in your life that are hurting your relationships and holding you back. Before identifying the cycles that need to be broken, in section one, we must understand why we make the choices that hurt our hearts and relationships.

Then, in section two, we identify and address five of the most repeated cycles we've seen in our own family and the families of countless individuals we've pastored and coached over the last fifteen years. At the end of each chapter, we will give you a Cycle-Breaking Prayer. Each prayer is to help you identify the cycle, surrender it to God, and start something new.

The journey won't be easy, but it will be worth it. We can't wait to see what God does as we discover how one choice can redeem what's been broken and help you step into God's preferred future.

Thank you for trusting us with your journey to healing and wholeness. You've already made the first choice that can lead to change—reading this book.

Grace and Peace,

Justin and Trisha

Part One

DÉJÀ VU ALL OVER AGAIN

1

WHY DO I DO WHAT I DON'T WANT TO DO?

Justin Davis

My parents married fifteen days after I was born. My mom was eighteen years old, and my dad was twenty-one. My mom got pregnant in high school, and though she graduated, her pregnancy derailed any college plans. My dad was great with his hands. After graduating from high school, he got a job as an auto mechanic. He also did other odd jobs through most of my childhood.

We were a low-income family. We were often on food stamps, shopped for school clothes at yard sales, and routinely borrowed money from my grandparents to cover unexpected expenses. I remember standing in line with my mom to get government cheese and bread. A few years after I was born, my sister, Meredith, was born. A few years after Meredith, my brother Jacob was born, and then, finally, a few years after Jacob, my brother Jonah was born.

A family of six, we never went on vacation. My dad couldn't afford to take time off because he was an hourly employee. If he wasn't clocking in, he wasn't getting paid. In my mind, people who went on vacation were rich. I was in awe of the kids in my class who went to a Florida beach on spring break or to Disney World over Christmas vacation.

We did go camping a few weekends each summer. When I was in fifth grade, we went to the North American Christian Convention in St. Louis, Missouri. Several thousand Christians from all over the country gathered for this annual convention of Christian Churches and Churches of Christ. There were plenary sessions throughout the day with powerful worship and special speakers from our movement's (we weren't allowed to call it a "denomination") biggest and most influential churches. There were also breakout sessions on different topics and church leadership training.

My dad took off work for a few days, and we made the four-hour drive from Crawfordsville, Indiana, to St. Louis. We couldn't afford to stay in a hotel, so we borrowed a pop-up camper to stay at a campground just outside of the city. We didn't have much money to eat out, so we packed food we could eat at the campground.

The best part of the convention for me was the Kid's Track. The Kid's Track was a daily kids' activity while parents were in the breakout sessions. For a few days, I felt like a rich kid. Up to that point in my life, I hadn't been out of the state of Indiana. Indianapolis was the only big city I'd been in, and I'd never had the feeling of being a tourist.

The Kid's Track was essentially a tour of some of St. Louis's best kid-friendly attractions. We went up in the Gateway Arch and looked across the Mississippi River. We went to the St. Louis Zoo— the first time I'd ever been to a zoo. I went to my first water park. I was living the lifestyle of the rich and famous. It was the biggest and best three-day vacation of my young life.

A few years later, when all four of us kids were in school, my mom started working part-time in my middle school cafeteria. She was on the same school schedule as us, so it was the perfect job. Her added income started to give us more financial margin.

In my freshman year of high school, my parents surprised us with a spring break trip to Chicago. Their tax return that year was a good one, and they used part of it to treat us to a family vacation. We were only going to be in Chicago for a few days, but we were staying in a hotel for the first time in my life. It was going to be an epic vacation.

There is much to do in Chicago, and my mom devised a great plan—the Museum of Science and Industry, the Shedd Aquarium, and a Chicago Bulls basketball game at the old Chicago Stadium. This was in 1988, when Michael Jordan was taking the NBA—and the country—by storm. I'd just finished my freshman year basketball season, and while I couldn't afford to buy Air Jordan basketball shoes, I had about every Michael Jordan poster in existence. I couldn't wait to see him play in person.

Chicago was about a three-hour drive from our house in Crawfordsville. On the first day of our trip, we drove to the city, found our hotel (which was more like a motel), and got settled. I remember driving through a Chicago neighborhood and seeing a pickup game of basketball in a park. My dad pulled over and asked if I wanted to play a game of Chicago pickup basketball. We all got out of the car and walked over to the courts. I waited what seemed like an eternity to get picked up on a team. My whole family sat there and watched me run up and down with the city of Chicago in the background. It was like I was in a movie.

The next day was our only full day in the city. We went to the Museum of Science and Industry during the day and the Bulls game that evening. We were so high up in the stands I could only assume the guy scoring all the points was Michael Jordan. But nosebleed seats were still in Chicago Stadium to see the GOAT play in person. It was a night I'll never forget.

The following day, my dad and I got up early to get breakfast for everyone. We rarely ate out, and when we did, it was a special occasion. We went through the drive-thru at McDonald's and got Egg McMuffins, hotcakes and sausage, and sausage, egg, and cheese biscuits. My all-time favorite breakfast was the Egg McMuffin. There was something special about how they cooked the eggs into a perfect circle. The Canadian bacon was perfectly steamed, and the cheese melted magically into the warm English muffin. I ordered two.

I scarfed down both McMuffins on our way back to the hotel. At the hotel, my mom and siblings ate their breakfast. Then, we all got ready to check out of the hotel, go to the Shedd Aquarium, and then head home.

As we packed the car, I started feeling dizzy. My stomach was achy and gassy, and I had to go to the bathroom. Clearly, my two Egg McMuffins were disagreeing with me. I ran into the hotel bathroom, and it seemed the McMuffins were running right through me. For a few minutes after, I felt better. But by the time I got in the car to go to the aquarium, I had gone from an upset stomach to full-on nausea. I felt like I was going to throw up. When we got to the aquarium, I sprinted to the bathroom and vomited in one of the stalls. As a sympathy puker, I won't go into details and risk making you feel sick, but I will say that every ounce of those Egg McMuffins revisited me that day.

My dad and I walked out of the bathroom, and my mom and siblings stood there looking at me like I'd just rained on their parade. My mom suggested we go on home since I wasn't feeling well. But my dad, who was recounting all the money we had just spent to get into the aquarium, had another idea. He said, "Justin is a big boy. He can lie down on one of the benches here in the lobby while we walk through with the other kids." My siblings were all for it, but my mom wasn't so sure. This was the late 1980s, before Amber Alerts. In those days, pictures of kids who went missing were put on milk cartons. (Google it.) I assumed that would be my fate.

My mom protested at first, but then someone in this conspiracy to get me kidnapped came up with another plan. A few yards away, an older lady was sitting on a cushioned bench by herself. My parents approached her and asked if anyone was with her. She said she was with her family but didn't feel like walking, so she was sitting there while they walked through the aquarium. My dad explained that I wasn't feeling well and needed to rest for a few minutes while he and my mom walked through with the younger kids. He asked if I could lie down on the bench next to her. I assume she said yes, because they left me with that elderly woman on the bench.

I spent the rest of my day at the Shedd Aquarium either in the bathroom stall throwing up Egg McMuffin or laying my head next to an elderly lady's lap. My cruel and selfish family enjoyed the aquarium and then talked about it all the way home. My final memory of that trip is standing on the side of Interstate 65 on our way home, projecting the final remnants of the Egg McMuffins into the ditch next to the road.

Those Egg McMuffins I ate thirty-six years ago are the last ones I've eaten. I never have eaten, nor will I ever eat, another Egg McMuffin. It was a choice I made when I was fourteen years old that has guided and shaped my dietary choices to this day.

There are choices we make, and the consequences are so severe that we never make that decision again. We learn our lesson the first time. Our experience is so formative that it causes us to choose something new. The pain of that choice was a defining moment that changed everything.

As I look back at the relationships in my life, I wish that were true of all my destructive, dysfunctional, or painful choices. Most of the problems in my family growing up were the same problems repeated. The issues that have dissolved friendships or caused misunderstandings in my work relationships are the same issues repeated across seasons of life, multiple work environments, and locations. Many of the arguments and issues Trisha and I have had in our twenty-nine years of marriage are not new; they are repetitive, cyclical behavior patterns, communication habits, and choices.

Choices, Patterns, and Cycles

In 2013, Trisha and I released our first book, *Beyond Ordinary: When a Good Marriage Just Isn't Good Enough*—a he said / she said memoir about how, by God's grace, our marriage journeyed from extraordinary to ordinary to nightmarish and back again.

Beyond Ordinary is a transparent, raw look into our vision for our marriage and how the gradual breakdown of that vision led to inauthenticity, deception, sexual brokenness, and infidelity. But it's also the story of the redemption, healing, and forgiveness that's marked the last nineteen years of our life and marriage. We share some of that story here to shed light on the repeated dysfunctional choices that led to our separation and near divorce.

As we have traveled the country speaking, teaching, and working with people in all stages of life and relationships, we have noticed this: None of us struggles with anything new. Most of the issues that hold us back and damage our most important relationships involve repeated choices and behaviors that we don't know how to change or a feeling of hopelessness about choosing a different way.

Several times a year, after we teach at a marriage conference or speak at a church, a husband and wife approach our table and pull us aside. They share enough of their story to let us know that they've gone through—or are going through—something. Then they say something like, "We've tried counseling, reading books, date nights—but we always hit a wall. We continue to fight about the same things." We hear many of the same things from the couples we work with one on one.

According to relationship and marriage expert Dr. John Gottman, couples wait an average of six years of being unhappy before getting help.[1] So, by the time a couple comes to us to seek help, they've usually been dealing with the same problems for years, feeling like they're beating their head against a wall. They are usually frustrated, exhausted, and losing hope that anything in their relationship can change.

Many of the harmful or hurtful choices we make aren't immediately detrimental to our relationships. You might tell a lie to your parents to escape consequences, and they don't catch you in the lie. You might gossip about a friend in high school and have the emotional agility to simply move on to a new friendship. You might cheat on a test in chemistry class and pass with flying colors without the teacher knowing. You might look at pornography occasionally, and because your wife doesn't know, feel like you're getting away with it.

But choices become patterns, and patterns become repeated cycles that hurt our relationships and hold us back. Rita Mae Brown famously said, "Insanity is doing the same thing over and over and expecting different results."[2]

In his book *Necessary Endings*, Dr. Henry Cloud said, "Getting to the next level always requires ending something, leaving it behind, and moving on. Growth itself demands that we move on. Without the ability to end things, people stay stuck, never becoming who they are meant to be, never accomplishing all that their talents and abilities should afford them."[3]

Are there choices you want to stop making, but you don't know how or don't have the courage to follow through? When it comes to the relationships in your life, do you make the same choices and expect different results? Those repeated patterns can make us feel insane.

Cycles Didn't Start with You

What if some of the choices you make and patterns you repeat didn't start with you? What if your family of origin has some responsibility for the dysfunctional cycles you repeat? No matter how toxic or healthy your family of origin may be, there are deeply ingrained messages, habits, coping skills, behavior patterns, addictions, and relational assumptions that affect your relationships today. While it may feel offensive when your spouse says, "You are just like your father," or "You sound just like your mother," it probably has more than a grain of truth to it.

We often underestimate the deep, unconscious imprint our families of origin leave on us. In his book *Emotionally Healthy Spirituality*, pastor and author Pete Scazzero traces one biblical family and shows that while God's blessing was passed down from generation to generation, so were destructive behavior patterns and repeated sins.

A Pattern of Lying in Each Generation

- Abraham lied twice about Sarah.
- Isaac and Rebekah's marriage was characterized by lies.

- Jacob lied to almost everyone; his name means "deceiver."
- Ten of Jacob's children lied about Joseph's death, faking a funeral and keeping a "family secret" for over ten years.

Favoritism by at Least One Parent in Each Generation

- Abraham favored Ishmael.
- Isaac favored Esau.
- Jacob favored Joseph and later Benjamin.

Brothers Experiencing a Cutoff in Each Generation

- Isaac and Ishmael (Abraham's sons) were cut off from one another.
- Jacob fled his brother Esau and was completely cut off for years.
- Joseph was cut off from his ten brothers for over a decade.

Poor Intimacy in the Marriages of Each Generation

- Abraham had a child out of wedlock with Hagar.
- Isaac had a terrible relationship with Rebekah.
- Jacob had two wives and two concubines.[4]

Without identifying, acknowledging, and submitting our familial patterns to God to bring transformation and healing, we are likely to repeat them.

In her book *I Thought It Was Just Me (but It Isn't)*, Brené Brown said, "Family messages die hard. And many times, they're very insidious. The messages become part of the fabric of our families. Until we can recognize and understand why and how they influence our lives, we just keep living by them and passing them down to the next generation."[5]

What is more crazy is that the choices we make are often unhealthy, hurtful, or harmful to the relationship, and we make that choice anyway. We know the lie will destroy trust, but we lie anyway. We know resentment limits our ability to love, but we are bitter anyway. We know a harsh word will wound a friendship, but we unleash it anyway. We know a hookup will cause us to feel shame, but we hook up anyway. We know another shopping spree on our credit card will increase our debt, but we shop anyway. We know sending a text or Facebook message to an old high school flame will hurt our marriage, but we hit send anyway. We don't want to hurt our most precious relationships, but we do it anyway.

Why do we do what we don't want to do? Wounding relationships by making choices against God's best isn't unique to you. Everyone struggles with it. One of Jesus' most influential followers in human history struggled with the same thing.

In Romans, the apostle Paul said:

> I do not understand what I do. For what I want to
> do I do not do, but what I hate I do. And if I do what

I do not want to do, I agree that the law is good. As it is, it is no longer I myself who do it, but it is sin living in me. For I know that good itself does not dwell in me, that is, in my sinful nature. For I have the desire to do what is good, but I cannot carry it out. For I do not do the good I want to do, but the evil I do not want to do—this I keep on doing. Now if I do what I do not want to do, it is no longer I who do it, but it is sin living in me that does it.

So I find this law at work: Although I want to do good, evil is right there with me. (Rom. 7:15–21 NIV)

As you read these words from Paul, you may, like me, resonate with the tension he was describing. I do what I don't want to do. You do what you don't want to do. I don't do what I want to do. You don't do what you want to do. It's not that we don't want to make different choices. But more than our desire is needed to break the cycles of our choices.

In my pastoral opinion, one of the biggest mistakes of the American Church has been our focus on the *fruit* of our choices and not the *root* of our choices. Just stop drinking. Just stop cursing. Stop lusting. Stop lying. Just stop sleeping around. Just read your Bible more. Just pray more. Just go to church more. We start with our behavior and hope that it will change our hearts. That philosophy (and, unfortunately, often theology) has left many of us stuck in cycles that continue to bring pain to our relationships and discouragement to our hearts.

A few years ago, Trish wanted to mulch the flower beds in our front yard. It was blazing hot outside; the last thing I wanted to do was landscape. I'm not too fond of manual labor. I'd rather hire someone to do this task, but Trish loves landscaping, so I saw it as an opportunity to be a good husband and build into my marriage.

I went to Home Depot and bought twelve bags of mulch. As I was unloading them, I noticed something I thought was odd. She wasn't just removing the old mulch from the flower beds to prepare for the new mulch (like I would have done); she was taking a shovel and digging up by the roots every weed and every blade of grass. At one point, I said, "That seems like a lot of work."

She said, "If I don't dig it up, it will return right back."

If we focus only on the "what" and not the "why" of our choices, we may be able to stop losing our temper for a short period of time. We may be able to tell the truth for a while. We may be able to avoid porn for a season. But until we identify and heal the "why," in times of stress, uncertainty, or pain, those choices will spring up from the root, whether or not we want them to.

Our Needs Drive Our Choices

Abraham Maslow was an American psychologist best known for creating a "hierarchy of needs," a theory of psychological health predicated on fulfilling innate human needs. His theory was first published in 1946 and included five levels of need: physiological, safety, love/belonging, self-esteem, and self-actualization. Since then, many psychologists have modified this theory. Some have expanded Maslow's needs to eight, while others have condensed them to three.

In a 2019 article, Dr. Brad Brenner identified five unmet needs that drive our choices. These needs resemble Maslow's hierarchy of needs from 1946.

1. Security
2. Approval
3. Control
4. Validation
5. Love[6]

While some of these terms are self-evident, others require more explanation to understand how they universally drive our choices.

Security

This basic human need includes the security of food, water, shelter, and physical protection. But it goes beyond our physical needs to include emotional security and safety.

Approval

Approval is a deep sense of belonging. It is more than just fitting in but living in a deep interpersonal connection with others. In *Psychology Today*, Kim Samuel wrote about belonging: "Belonging isn't just a connection to other people, but also to place, power, and purpose. The experience of belonging is about connectedness through community, rootedness in a place, a feeling of ownership in shared outcomes, and a sense of mission with others."[7]

Control

Control in its healthiest form is responsibility. When we live from a place of wholeness, we take responsibility for our actions, choices, and decisions. But when we experience trauma, then our need for control increases so we can protect ourselves from future traumatic experiences.

Validation

Validation is similar to approval but becomes more of a granular need for praise, attention, words of encouragement, and affirmation. In our social media–driven society, this need for validation has only increased as we receive dopamine hits with every Heart, Like, and Share.

Love

Our greatest fear in human relationships is that we won't be loved. Neglect, abandonment, criticism, and rejection all fly in the face of our desire and need to be loved. Many of the negative or hurtful choices we make reflect our desire to love and be loved by another person and our fear that the people we love most won't love us.

Every conscious decision comes from a desire to fill these five core needs. As you navigate decisions in the context of your relationships, your desire to do what is right seems less critical than filling these five basic needs. This is why you will lie to yourself and others if it means being loved. It's why you'll cheat on a test if it means being validated by your parents. It's why you'll promise your family you'll work less and be home more but continue to be a workaholic—not because you don't love your family, but because you feel a lack of security.

Some of the most destructive choices we make come from a place of healthy needs that have gone unmet or been distorted by traumatic events in our lives. We fall into a pattern, a cycle that, unless it is intentionally broken, repeats itself in each relationship and stage of life.

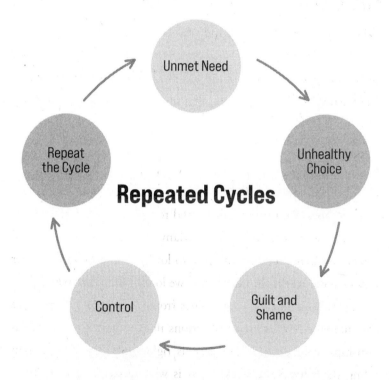

Out of our unmet needs, we make unhealthy choices that hurt our relationships and hold us back. As a result of our choices, we naturally feel guilty. After guilt hits our hearts, we live out of shame, and we try to control our behavior. Our desire to control is driven by the hurt we've brought to a relationship with our choices. However, our ability to control only exists to the extent that we can try harder to make better choices. When we run out of willpower or the guilt trip we're on, we repeat the cycle.

The Two-Headed Monster of Guilt and Control

In later chapters, we will discuss this passage from Genesis 3 and unpack the idea of guilt and shame. We see guilt affect Adam and Eve's relationship with God and one another immediately after they choose to eat the fruit from the Tree of the Knowledge of Good and Evil.

> At that moment their eyes were opened, and they suddenly felt shame at their nakedness. So they sewed fig leaves together to cover themselves.
>
> When the cool evening breezes were blowing, the man and his wife heard the LORD God walking about in the garden. So they hid from the LORD God among the trees. Then the LORD God called to the man, "Where are you?"
>
> He replied, "I heard you walking in the garden, so I hid. I was afraid because I was naked."
>
> "Who told you that you were naked?" the LORD God asked. "Have you eaten from the tree whose fruit I commanded you not to eat?"

> The man replied, "It was the woman you gave
> me who gave me the fruit, and I ate it."
>
> Then the LORD God asked the woman, "What
> have you done?"
>
> "The serpent deceived me," she replied. "That's
> why I ate it." (Gen. 3:7–13)

Guilt is more about being caught than being known. Guilt leads to hiddenness, blame, isolation, and shame. Because guilt is usually associated with our behavior and not our heart, we respond to guilt with other unhealthy choices. Rather than take ownership, we blame. Rather than be honest with ourselves and others, we hide or deceive. We isolate ourselves relationally rather than trust others with the truth about us. We begin to negotiate with ourselves that we'll never do that again. We'll never talk like that to our husband again. We'll never date someone like that person again. We'll never look at an image like that again. We'll never distort the truth again.

Bartering and negotiating with ourselves and God leads to the next stage of repeated cycles: control.

Control is about you and your ability to avoid an unhealthy choice again. You tell yourself you just need to try harder. You need an internet filter. You need an accountability partner. You need to be a better parent. You need to listen more. You need to control your temper. You need to work less and be more present at home. You need to stop flirting with your coworker.

If you are in a dating or marriage relationship, you might try to control your partner's behavior so they don't hurt or disappoint you again. They've made an unhealthy choice, demonstrated regret, and now you are going to control their behavior so you aren't hurt again.

Control of yourself and especially of others is an illusion. While self-control is a fruit of the Spirit, it doesn't refer to your ability to control but your willingness to allow the Holy Spirit to develop self-control in you.

When we experience regret and white-knuckle our way through control, we end up exhausted and defeated, which causes us to repeat the cycle of our unmet needs.

You *can* break the cycle. You can choose something different. You can make one choice that will bring healing to your heart and transformation to your relationships. You can get out of the cycle of insanity of doing the same thing repeatedly, expecting different results.

The Path to Healing

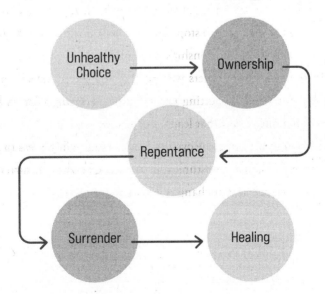

Healing is organic and messy. It's not a formula to figure out, but a rugged and uncomfortable path to walk. Sometimes, on this path, you feel like you're making great strides. Other times you feel like you are taking two steps forward and three steps back. This isn't a race you're running. The fastest time doesn't win. Being committed to the journey is more important than the speed at which you travel. God is restoring you and remaking you each step of the way, even if it doesn't feel like it.

Remember when Adam and Eve sinned against God, and hid behind fig leaves?

God went searching. Not to punish them, but to cover them. Not to condemn them, but to restore them. As we start this journey together, we're going to share with you personal experiences and biblical examples of how you are often one choice away from change. This book isn't a guarantee you won't make unhealthy or sinful choices. Even the apostle Paul struggled to make the right choices. But this book will help you stop repeating the same mistakes that are hurting you and the relationships you hold dear.

In the next few chapters we will discover the power of understanding our wounds, getting past our past, grieving what is lost, and making one choice that leads to change.

The key to breaking the cycle is found in our willingness to give up control and adopt a posture of surrender. Choosing to surrender is the *one choice* that will change everything.

CYCLE-BREAKING PRAYER

Jesus, I come to you with a heart longing for true surrender. I've tried to control my life and it's only led to repeated cycles that are holding me back and hurting my relationships. I can't break these patterns alone. I need your help. As I go on this journey, help me see the behaviors that hinder my growth and are damaging those I love most. I surrender my fears, doubts, and the need to manage everything. I choose to give all of this to you. Guide, transform, and lead me into renewed purpose and restored relationships. In Jesus' name, amen.

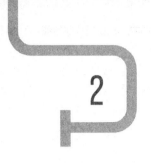

GET PAST
YOUR PAST

Trisha Davis

Your past, my past, and God's past—we all have a past—that's the good news. The bad news is that's where our shared connection ends. Your past and my past are as different as our DNA. God's past—well, that's a mystery all its own. Our history can anchor us to dysfunction or give us rose-colored glasses of the glory days past. No matter how we view our past, we all struggle to some extent with how the past influences our present and shapes our future.

Have you ever reminisced with a friend or family member about a shared experience only to realize that each of you remembers it differently? You banter back and forth about how it all unfolded, but you have to agree to disagree because you both believe your version is the right one. The truth is that even though we share experiences, we don't always perceive or experience them in the same way. Your vantage point is just that—it's yours.

I grew up with my sister, Julie, who's three years older, and my brother, Frankie, who is sixteen months younger. When the three of us get together, you can count on two things: laughter and storytelling. You can also count on hearing three different versions of the same story. We moved a handful of times as kids, so we often frame our childhood stories through the houses we lived in. One of our favorite houses—which holds some of our best memories—was the Prospect Street house.

The Prospect Street house sat at the top of a hill, and the bottom of the hill intersected with three different streets. When it rained for long periods of time, the bottom of the hill flooded, and we, along with other neighborhood kids, would swim in it—for hours. Remember, this was the '80s, so we didn't have Wi-Fi, Google, or social media for anyone to tell us how insanely gross this was; we were blissfully unaware. But the memories created in our mud pool made for epic storytelling.

For several years, my sister and I were the only girls on that street. It should've been called "Boy Lane," because of the abundance of boys who lived on our block. It also explains why we were swimming in our "neighborhood pool" at the bottom of the hill.

One day, the neighborhood boy gang came to where I was playing in my yard. One of them said, "Tell us where you're going tonight."

I replied, "Why?"

He insinuated that the boy gang wanted to know.

I relented, and with a strong side-eye, said, "I'm going to *turch.*" And they all roared with laughter.

Although I knew I struggled with pronouncing certain words, I didn't realize my speech impediment was noticeable enough for others to tease me about it.

Many years later, I saw one of those boys from our neighborhood at a friend's wedding. Sure enough, as soon as I saw him, the *first* thing out of his mouth was, "Hey, are you still going to 'turch'?" I was so taken aback that, to this day, I can't remember how I responded. But I do remember how I felt—angry and embarrassed.

Looking back at that moment, I realize that he remembered these childhood moments from the view of a little boy teasing and annoying a little girl. But I remembered his words as playing a part in defining how I saw myself for years to come. This story highlights two significant barriers we often struggle with to overcome our past.

Overcoming Different Perspectives

The first barrier to overcoming our past is failing to recognize that the same story can be viewed from different perspectives.

For example, imagine two middle-school-aged siblings experiencing the loss of their father. During the funeral, an adult tells one sibling they should be grateful for the time with their dad and tells the other how sorry they are that their dad isn't here anymore. Now, as grown adults, whenever they talk about their father's funeral, one sibling doesn't remember feeling sad, while the other recalls feeling lonely. But instead of honoring each other's experience with their dad's funeral, each minimizes the other's reaction, because they can't understand why the other would feel that way.

Think about your past. Are there moments in your history when you've expressed how others made you feel only to be told you were wrong? "That's not how it happened!" You may know in your bones how a painful event played out, and you can't get over how clueless and dismissive family or friends are about how that event shaped your life.

Are there moments from your past where a friend or family member has unfairly placed the burden of guilt, blame, or shame on you for a decision they believe you were responsible for or didn't handle well, even though you don't think you did anything wrong?

When we fail to recognize that the same shared experience can be viewed from different perspectives, and we believe our vantage point is the *only* vantage point, it creates cycles of unresolved relational conflict. When we allow another person's perspective to be the only valid way of understanding a difficult moment in our past, it creates cycles of unhealed wounds. So how do you break through this barrier?

There is no right or wrong way to remember your past. In fact, recognizing that the same story can be viewed from different perspectives allows you to acknowledge your own pain—without feeling like you have to defend or explain it away—and begin the process of healing. When you accept someone else's perspective as just that—their perspective—you stop becoming defensive or dismissive of their feelings. In fact, sometimes seeing your pain through another person's lens can create a layer of understanding you couldn't have discovered from your view. When you willingly acknowledge their viewpoint, it makes them feel seen and heard, but it doesn't necessarily make them right. A willingness to listen without defense fosters healing in your relationship.

Internal Messages

The second barrier to overcoming our past is failing to recognize the messages we've internalized from the words of others.

Words spoken over us leave lasting messages. But too often, we don't trace the messages that trapped us in unhealthy cycles back to where we received them.

To continue the previous example, one sibling was told to be grateful for the time with their dad. Although the words were meant to console, the message received was, "Being sad is bad; being grateful is good." Words spoken over them at a vulnerable moment created an unhealthy cycle of believing that sadness indicates a lack of gratitude, rather than being a sign of healthy grief. This message shaped their definition of grief and caused them to spend much of their adult life stuffing their grief, but never understanding why. As a result, when their sibling criticizes them for not showing sadness, it creates a disconnect and leads to defensiveness.

The other sibling was told, "I'm sorry that your dad isn't here anymore." Words meant to acknowledge the child's loss gave the child the message, "Because your dad is gone, you are alone and on your own." Those words created a cycle of unhealthy independence, causing them to try to do life all on their own. To have the other sibling criticize them for not being there for them creates a disconnect and leads to unresolved conflict.

The heartbreak in this example is that neither sibling did anything wrong; words spoken over them turned into messages, and those messages became unhealthy cycles.

Words spoken over us leave lasting messages, and *words* become *messages* that become *cycles*.

Throughout the Bible, we can see words become messages that become cycles. In Genesis 3, Satan said four words to Eve that changed the course of humanity: "Did God really say …?" Those four words spoken over Eve turned into a message that she wasn't enough. It was a message that trapped her in a cycle of sin that we all struggle with to this day.

Words Become Messages That Become Cycles

Judges 6 opens with a strong statement about the state of God's people: "The Israelites did evil in the LORD's sight. So the LORD handed them over to the Midianites for seven years" (v. 1). Sadly, this isn't the first—or the last—time in the Old Testament that these words were used to describe the Israelites. Since they had abandoned God to worship other gods, God put them under the rule of the Midianites.

The movie *Dune* can help us picture what unfolded between the Israelites and Midianites. Let me give you the CliffsNotes version. *Dune* is set in a futuristic period in which humanity is spread across multiple planets and ruled by a high counsel and an evil emperor.

Each planet and its people are associated with a "house." There are the House Atreides, House Harkonnen, House Corrino, and

House Fenring, to name a few. Referring to people groups as houses was also common in the Old Testament. For example, when the tribes of Manasseh and Ephraim joined together, they were known as the house of Joseph.[1] Those who lived under the rule of King Saul (the first king of Israel) were identified as the house of Saul.

The Midianites were like House Fremen on Arrakis. They were desert people and descendants of Abraham's second wife, Keturah. Like the various houses in *Dune*, the Israelites and the Midianites were constantly at war with each other, and at the beginning of Judges 6, the Midianites were winning.

Desperate for help, the Israelites cried out to God. One might assume God would send a mighty hero from the mightiest of the twelve tribes, like in *Dune*, where Paul Atreides, who is of royal blood, is chosen to become the savior of all the planets by saving Arrakis. But no, God decided to go in the exact opposite direction. God chose a guy named Gideon.

Gideon, unlike Paul Atreides, didn't come from a royal family. In fact, he was the least of the least. He came from the clan of Abiezer, the weakest clan of the tribe of Manasseh, the least of the twelve tribes of Judah. Gideon was a guy that not even the kids at the playground would pick.

As the story goes, God sent an angel (that scholars contend was God himself) to tell Gideon the amazing news that God had handpicked him to rescue all twelve tribes of Israel. "The angel of the LORD appeared to him and said, 'Mighty hero, the LORD is with you!'" (Judg. 6:12). Gideon didn't know the plan yet, and God addressed him as a "mighty hero."

We just went from *Dune* to Marvel. No big deal.

Gideon handled this news with the utmost confidence and clarity: "'But Lord,' Gideon replied, 'how can I rescue Israel? My clan is the weakest in the whole tribe of Manasseh, and I am the least in my entire family!'" (Judg. 6:15).

Gideon's community and culture told him that, even though he was part of God's chosen people, he was still the least in his community, tribe, and family. Words become messages that become cycles, and the message Gideon received was that he was insignificant. Because he saw himself as inferior, he felt inadequate and lived with the belief that he couldn't contribute at any level. Gideon's message of insignificance trapped him in a cycle of unworthiness, affecting his present and, ultimately, his future.

Gideon and I would have made the best of friends, because on that day those boys laughed at how I talked, it sent a very clear message to me: I was stupid. Being labeled stupid wasn't new for me; it was more like the final nail in the coffin of my confidence.

People tried to tell me I was smart. My friend Deon convinced me to participate in our elementary school spelling bee. He knew I couldn't say words right, so why did he think I could spell them? But Deon, who was in the "gifted" program, was convinced I had it in me—and he was smart, so I trusted him.

You're probably already stressed about how this story ends, and you should be.

I reluctantly participated in that spelling bee, and in the first round, I got the word *bus*, which I knew how to say and spell! So, I proudly stood up on the stage of our school cafetorium, walked to the microphone, and said in front of the entire student body, "Bus … B … U … S … [long pause] … S."

And EVERYONE laughed, except for Deon. On my walk of shame back to my seat, he said, "You'll get it next time." Yes, that is what he said, and to know him is to say, "That sounds like Deon."

This story represents one of many instances where I knew, deep down, that I was stupid. Words became messages that became cycles, and my message, like Gideon's, was, "I'm inadequate." My cycle was unworthiness, because I thought I wasn't smart enough to be great at anything.

To break cycles in our lives, we must first discover our messages, which requires some trips down memory lane. Many of us believe the lie that we don't need to revisit the past because we can't change it. Others work hard to improve themselves to avoid returning to the problematic places their past can take them. However, if we don't acknowledge the words that became ingrained messages, we fail to recognize the cycles of dysfunction in which we are entrapped.

H. Norman Wright listed four reasons we avoid confronting the past.

1. Some don't want to admit that what happened to them happened.

2. Some believe if they admit to the hurt and pain of the past, they are in some way different or damaged and not useful to others. They want to see themselves as okay, but they don't. They definitely don't want others to know, because

they don't want to be judged or offered unwanted advice.

3. Some are afraid to confront the painful past. That's understandable. There is fear that experiencing that pain again might be too much to bear.

4. There is also the fear that experiencing the past may require change, which opens the door to failure.[2]

Phew, if that list stirred up emotions for you, you're not alone. No one in their right mind wants to revisit the past and unearth old pain. No one wants unsolicited advice or to be judged. No one wants to change today when it won't alter the past but could lead to future failure.

Confronting Your Past

But imagine flipping the script on our fears and turning them into a process. Admitting what happened to you doesn't give the past power. In fact, confronting your past can give your present a path to discover more about yourself, allowing you to heal and grow.

Think of it as *excavating* your past rather than exposing your past.

Maybe you can't recall experiencing any major traumatic events, so you don't feel the need to become an archaeologist of your past. And yet, there are cycles you are stuck in but can't seem to put your finger on how you got there. Or maybe for you, excavating your past would be like digging up a T-rex. It's just too big, too much to handle. And yet, the ground under which it's buried continues to be the foundation you can't stop building on.

This is where we find Gideon. He didn't share any significant events of his past. He was not David who slayed a giant or Moses who led the Israelites to an impassable sea with the Egyptian army chasing after them. There was no need for Gideon to excavate his past because there was no giant, no sea to be found. However, his life had been built from deeply embedded cultural norms that had cemented his family, his community, and his nation as the least of the least. And Gideon had accepted it as the truth.

After Gideon gave God his dissertation about why he wasn't enough, God responded with words that carried a very clear message: "I will be with you. And you will destroy the Midianites as if you were fighting against one man" (Judg. 6:16). God told Gideon that he was enough.

But Gideon could only hear the message of inadequacy, which trapped him in the cycle of unworthiness. So, he asked God for a sign to prove it was God speaking. God agreed, and Gideon went home quickly to cook God a meal. But before he left, he asked God to stay until Gideon came back. God replied, "I will stay here until you return." God's message to Gideon was, "I'm with you. I will stay."

Gideon returned with his offering meal and found that God had kept his word. God then told him his plan to defeat the Midianites and clothed him with his power. Note that God called Gideon a mighty hero before giving him the plans or power. He stayed as Gideon concocted an offering God didn't ask for. But Gideon was so entrenched in his cycle of inadequacy that, even then, he still needed proof that God was for him. Instead of being "all in" with his new hero status and having God's presence and power, he asked God to prove himself—two more times. Gideon needed reassurance that God really was going to stay and empower him.

It's easy to caricature people in the Bible, but Gideon was a real dude with real issues. Gideon didn't doubt God's power; he doubted God would use his power through him. What I see in this passage is what we all crave from God—reassurance that God will be there for us when we're good, bad, indifferent, frustrated, depressed, elated, overwhelmed, on top of the world, or on the bottom of the food chain. We want what Gideon wants—reassurance.

So why didn't God's words move Gideon to see himself differently? Because words become messages that become cycles. Cycles can sift out the truth and trap us in the same lies. Gideon sifted God's words through his cycle of unworthiness and doubt.

Rather than confronting his past and surrendering it to God, Gideon was living from his past and therefore needed God to prove his new hero status. He was looking for reassurance that he was significant, capable of leading his entire community, and worthy to be a winner. Cycles can lead to narratives that get buried so deep within us that the narratives become the stories we live.

Maybe you picked up this book because you, like Gideon, can't recall a large-T trauma like some of your friends or family can. You don't have a giant-slaying or sea-parting experience, so confronting your past doesn't seem necessary. And yet, you are stuck in cycles and can't seem to figure out how you got there—which honestly makes sense. But just because you don't have a large-T trauma event in your past, it doesn't diminish your less dramatic childhood wounds.

Whether it's a neighborhood boy making fun of you, a coach who said you'll never be good enough, or a family member declaring you the least in your family, words carry power.

Maybe you know the date, the time, the smell, and the clothes you were wearing when your big, bad, terrible event happened—and the fear of dragging it all back up feels foolish. Maybe you've risked sharing that memory with a friend or family member only to be given harmful or unwanted advice. You've tried talking to a pastor or a counselor, but the excavation was too painful.

Regardless of what camp you find yourself in, we all fear being ostracized by our family, community, or way of life. The "what-ifs" carry too much risk. We think, *I don't want relationships to change. I'd rather live with my dysfunctional status quo than make a risky move toward change.*

> It is worth noting that developing post-trauma symptoms is by no means an indication of psychological weakness or congenital deficiency. In fact, these difficulties typically develop due to the individual engaging in avoidance behaviors. Such behaviors are engaged to conceal distress with the belief that not addressing what has happened will free the individual of their emotional pain. Avoidance is also engaged so as not to reveal any "weaknesses" or difficulty to others. By most standards, these individuals would likely be referred to as "strong-minded" or "tough"; their ability to experience such hardships and rise above them would be deemed honorable.[3]

Gideon was at this crux to break his cycle when God asked him to take action and become a mighty hero. He had to decide if he was going to remain the same—head buried, living an "it is what it is" life—or make *one* choice that could change everything.

> That night the LORD said to Gideon, "Take the second bull from your father's herd, the one that is seven years old. Pull down your father's altar to Baal, and cut down the Asherah pole standing beside it." (Judg. 6:25)

Before Gideon moved forward, God's first directive was to go back and break a generational cycle passed down through his father. God told him to tear down idols that represented false gods from other "houses." This public act would cause relational strife in the worst way.

> The people said to each other, "Who did this?" And after asking around and making a careful search, they learned that it was Gideon, the son of Joash.
>
> "Bring out your son," the men of the town demanded of Joash. "He must die for destroying the altar of Baal and for cutting down the Asherah pole." (Judg. 6:29–30)

Change is risky. But you won't see those three words used as an inspirational quote on anyone's mantel.

Breaking cycles begins with *one* choice: **Confront your past.**

Is it risky? Yes. Gideon risked being excommunicated at best, killed at worst. But Gideon chose to confront his past by making one choice to break free from it in his present. He trusted God.

The choices in our past create the patterns we repeat unless we confront them and choose something different. Before we can receive, we have to surrender. Surrender is a posture of willingness and an openness to confront the past so you can discover the words that became your messages and cycles. Surrender in this context isn't about shame or wrongdoing; it's about excavating your past to find freedom in your present.

God is inviting you to journey to your past and confront it head-on by surrendering it with confidence and clarity from your perspective. You don't have to accept someone else's point of view. Even if they remember past events exactly the same, how those events shaped you will be unique to you. You will remember it differently from those who raised you and those who have shared experiences with you—and that's okay. Everyone has a unique perspective from their own vantage point. Confronting your past is surrendering truth and untruth and gaining freedom, wisdom, and acceptance over what was but doesn't have to be. It's discovering your wounds and the messages they created. Identifying your wounds allows you to address and heal them, preventing them from controlling your present or repeating in the future.

Start with One Choice

So how do you start? When you think about your past, what wounds come to mind? Take a minute and think about moments in your childhood where words were spoken to you or over you. What messages did they leave with your heart and mind? If you could take all those words and accumulate them into one word, what would it be? If nothing comes immediately to mind, don't stress. This isn't a onetime moment of revelation; it's a process. The heart of this book is to guide you through this process.

I'm not sure if Gideon broke his cycle of inadequacy. You can read the rest of the story in Judges 7–8 and decide for yourself. For my story, I have spent most of my adult life on a quest to break my own cycles, beginning with my cycle of unworthiness. For years, my Asherah poles were my age and worthiness. I was too young, too old, and never enough.

In 2022, I made a choice to go back to college to complete my bachelor's degree at age forty-seven. It had been a dream of mine to get my bachelor's degree. But what if I was too old? And what if the neighborhood boys were right? What if I couldn't speak and write? What if I couldn't learn and write at a collegiate level?

If you've read our first book, *Beyond Ordinary*, that last sentence may have thrown you for a loop. But it's very common for people to refer to *Beyond Ordinary* as Justin's book. I once had a prominent author I greatly respect ask me who my ghostwriter was for *Beyond Ordinary* (hand on face emoji here). I guess my ability to write a book was just a fluke. Maybe I'm not really an author.

Words become messages that become cycles.

But I made the decision to confront my past and excavate this message of unworthiness that caused me to build Asherah poles of inadequacy. I tore those suckers down and went back to school to finish my undergrad degree. It took me two years but I'm officially a graduate of the class of 2024—and with a 4.0 GPA. The old me would diminish this achievement so as to not offend you or to come off like I'm bragging—because my old cycle would remind me that you are more worthy than me to receive this gift. Or, even worse, I would dumb down this achievement just in case the neighborhood boys and the famous author are still right—I'm not really smart, and this achievement was a fluke.

But I worked hard for my degree. I've cried hard tears (just ask my family) over assignments. I've also squealed with elation when I finished a class. School was my one choice to break my cycle of unworthiness. This accomplishment isn't the win; the win is that I trusted God to help me through—and he did.

My hope and prayer is to inspire you to tear down your own Asherah poles.

Your story, my story, and God's story are about a choice—to go back to go forward. Confronting your past is a choice to surrender to what was and experience what can be. We can break ties with our messages and cycles. It begins with this one choice: confront your past.

CYCLE-BREAKING PRAYER

Jesus, I come to you seeking clarity and courage to identify the Asherah poles in my life—the idols and distractions that keep me from your best. These things cause me to repeat my past instead of healing from it. Help me surrender my past mistakes and release the burdens of regret. I want to embrace the future you have planned for me, full of hope and purpose. Be my guide and my strength as you bring transformation to my heart. In your name, amen.

3

THE MESSY MIDDLE

Trisha Davis

Picture pulling up to a large old house with a wraparound porch and windows for days. The house has been preserved with the utmost care. You start to take in the house's surroundings and notice a handful of cabins behind the main house and beautiful rolling hills as far as the eye can see. There are horses grazing, goats bleating, and a gentle wind blowing through the surrounding trees.

As you enter the old house, you are greeted with a warm smile by a person handing you a bottle of water and giving you directions to turn in your phone because there's no need for a phone here. You're handed a key and told your cabin number. You head to your cabin, still taking in all the beauty the place offers. You find your cabin, nervously open the door, and find it as beautiful on the inside as on the outside. With white linens, a soft bed, a small dresser, and a side table, it's a perfect place for rest and relaxation. But before you can take a nap, it's lunchtime.

The cafeteria is a three-minute walk, and you can see it from your cabin. It's a beautiful building with floor-to-ceiling windows. As you make your way to lunch, you see two horses in full gallop, playing, as other horses stand by and watch. You reach the cafeteria, and in keeping with the theme of this place, it's as beautiful on the inside as on the outside. You peruse the menu and realize the offerings seem a bit fancy—some even hard to say—but you grab your plate and find your seat, and the first bite is everything you'd hoped it would be and more.

Welcome to Trauma Camp.

Trauma Camp, aka Onsite, is located about forty minutes west of Nashville, Tennessee. Onsite offers an array of services provided by certified professionals in mental health. The "camp" I attended was eight days of meditations, psychoeducational lectures, six hours of experiential group therapy, and guided activities designed to help me heal.

It was circa 2021, and I was a mess. A. HOT. MESS.

I found myself at Trauma Camp via one of my best friends, Lindsey, who was the VP of marketing at Onsite. I called and asked her if it would be a good idea to bring my hot mess to one of their "camps," and without hesitation she said it would. So, just like a middle school girl whose BFF invites her to go to church camp, I signed up. Honestly, I had no idea what I had signed up for; I just knew I was desperate for help. I trusted Lindsey, and trust was in short supply in my world.

Have you ever noticed how messes always seem to be in the middle of everything? Maybe you've said to a roommate or family member, "Why are your clothes in the middle of the floor?" "Why did you leave dishes in the middle of the sink?" "Why did you put the toilet paper roll in the middle of the floor rather than the dispenser?" "Why did you park your car in the middle of the driveway?" Why are messes always in the way?

Taking that idea a bit further, why does life get messy at the worst possible time?

Why did the rain have to wreak havoc on my parade?

Why did the job fall through when I was just getting financially stable?

Why did my friendship go south right before a significant milestone?

Why is the mess always in the middle of what was and what could've been?

In January 2020, Hope City, the church plant we started in 2016, had grown to over six hundred people. We had moved into a large building that was home to a dying church. Hope City needed space, and the church that owned the building needed financial support. It was meant to be a win-win all around. There had even been talk of merging, but at that moment, both congregations were just grateful for one another. In February, as Hope City continued to grow, we ordered a hundred more chairs for the sanctuary. It was a sweet time in the life of our baby church.

With all the new people coming, we decided to do a grand reopening of the church. We sent out a ten-thousand-piece mailer to the community and invited them to join us for our grand reopening on March 15, 2020.

You read that right: March 15, 2020—the day the whole world shut down due to Covid-19.

Our church was on the cusp of being able to provide brand-new ministries. We had finally launched our youth ministry, and our small groups were growing like never before. We held our first live event—a sold-out event with our dear friend Annie—just one week prior to the shutdown. So much life and community were taking place. Why did Covid have to happen in the middle of it all?

Instead of March 15, 2020, being our grand reopening, it was more like our grand closing. The whole world was stuck in a messy middle that seemed to keep getting worse. I'm sure you have your own hard stories about your experience with this global messy middle. What I didn't foresee amidst the chaos of the global shutdown was that this was only the beginning of cascading closures for me and my family.

"Bless this mess" was the sign that was hanging over the sink in the kitchen of our new rental. It was another messy middle that was devastating for our kids. When we bought our house in 2015, our kids were eighteen, sixteen, and thirteen. Two years later, we adopted our son and daughter at ages nine and seven. Because of the ages of our kids, that house is the last house in the history of the Davis family where every kid had their own room and memories of living together. Much as my siblings loved the Prospect house, our kids loved the Briarwood house.

So, when we told them, in 2021, that we wanted to sell the house, they all wanted us to keep it. But they also knew what was at stake and that it was still just a house. We convinced ourselves and them that God would "Bless this mess." The church was struggling to get people to come back and to continue tithing. Justin and I were both on staff at the church full-time, but to keep our other staff members from taking pay cuts, we both took turns not getting paid throughout 2021.

Justin started doing more recruiting for banks, a job he's continued to do off and on since 2009. My adjunct teaching pastor position at another church abruptly ended. Our speaking schedule had waned due to Covid, and while we continued to have some speaking engagements, it wasn't enough. We had to decide—close the church or sell our home. We chose the latter. In May 2021, we sold our house and used the equity to keep us and the church alive. It was a messy middle that we knew God would bless. Unfortunately, our mess was about to go from "clothes in the middle of the floor" to "Hurricane Katrina."

In the Middle of Everything

Messes in the middle of everything can powerfully affect our ability to keep moving. It's a weird in-between of not wanting to deal with the messy middle, so we shove it in closets and under rugs—and yet, it's all we think about. It's what psychologist Susan David calls the "three-teeter-totter principle."

> When we're juggling so many complexities that Superman and Wonder Woman together couldn't

> get it all done working double shifts, when we're walking on eggshells in an unpredictable relationship, we can become stressed in ways that inhibit our ability to be creative, to be appropriately responsive, and to thrive. Staying emotionally agile requires us to find the equilibrium between overconfidence on the one hand and overchallenge on the other.[1]

In Genesis 2, "The LORD God made all kinds of trees grow out of the ground—trees that were pleasing to the eye and good for food. In the middle of the garden were the tree of life and the tree of the knowledge of good and evil" (v. 9 NIV). The two most important trees in the history of mankind were planted by God smack-dab in the middle of the most treasured and sacred land, called Eden. The Tree of Life was just that; it was life giving, and it was God's first choice for all of mankind. The Tree of the Knowledge of Good and Evil was full of a lifetime of messy middles where both good *and* evil reside.

God made a bunch of trees "pleasing to the eye" that bore delicious food. The word *eden* means "pleasant, pleasure, delight." God's desire for us is found in verse 25: "Adam and his wife were both naked, and they felt no shame" (NIV). They were flourishing and thriving, not just because of the Tree of Life, but because they were living in an intimate, accepting, belonging, loving relationship with God—fully known and fully loved.

God knew that the Tree of Life was the best plan for living, so why ruin it by placing a tree full of hot messes next to the good tree?

Why plant it in the middle? Why not put it somewhere less conspicuous? The answer is the gift of choice. God's love was wrapped in the gift of choice. It wasn't a mistake on God's part to plant that mess of a tree in the middle of the garden. It was his intentional gift of choice—a choice to trust him and be loved by him.

The messy middle isn't life lived in the closet or under the rug. The messy middle isn't a place where we must hide or resign to the mindset that nothing can change. God knew what he was doing placing those trees in the garden. God knew that love wrapped in choice is the most powerful gift we can receive from him.

The Tree of the Knowledge of Good and Evil wasn't there for punishment; it was there so that Adam and Eve had a choice to choose him and to choose each other. And one fateful day, Adam and Eve chose the fruit of the messy tree. What is often left out of this narrative is that, although the mess of sin changed how we choose God, the goodness of God was and is equally there.

The goodness of the Tree of the Knowledge of Good and Evil is the opportunity to still choose God. But the choice is no longer between two trees; it's now between the teeter-totter of our messes.

Susan David put it this way:

> In life, the teeter-totter principle means finding that give-and-take, that place where competence and the comfort of the familiar exist in a kind of creative tension with the excitement and even the stress of the unknown. We get to that zone of optimal development in a very specific way: when we

> *live at the edge of our ability*, a place in which we're
> not overcompetent or complacent, but also not in
> so far over our heads that we're overwhelmed.[2]

The new choice sin brought into the picture is a choice to accept God's invitation; to live in his goodness while in the messy middle; to invite God into our familiar and our unknowns. The messy middle isn't something to just get over. It's learning and growing while you move through. But how does one move through? How do you grow when one day you're soaring so high you can almost feel the breath of God, only to find yourself the next day going through a dark tunnel with no end in sight?

In the summer of 2021, just weeks after selling our house, I had a conversation with my sister about the deep dive I had done into my family's ancestry through Ancestry.com two years prior. Because a whole generation on my dad's side of the family was starting to pass away, I wanted to start a family tree of the Lopez side of our family to capture their stories and learn more about the Hispanic origins of our family and culture. I also mentioned to her how strange it was that my heritage results showed no connections to the Lopez side of the family. I shared with her about asking our mom, who said she couldn't explain it either. At the time, I didn't understand the process of how Ancestry captured data, so for two years, I simply dismissed it—until my sister responded with questions of her own.

What started as an innocent conversation between me and my sister became a divesting storm of hiddenness and devastation. I went back to my DNA profile and discovered that the Lopez tree I was trying to connect to revealed that I was an NMP. Never heard of an NMP before? Me neither. NMP stands for Not My Parent.

My dad is a short Mexican man who has brown eyes and amazing black hair. I have blue eyes and blonde hair. I have spent my whole life explaining to people that I'm *not* the mailman's daughter. Every year in school, when my name was called, I had to explain to the teacher that my last name was indeed Lopez. But I was never fazed by it. EVER. Never once did I question whether my dad was my dad, because we are so much alike. We both like to work with our hands. We're athletic. We have stubby feet and a button nose. We're hard workers. So what if our skin, eyes, and hair are different colors? I was totally like my dad—until I wasn't.

This was a messy middle that I didn't see coming—or ending. My dad and I took a paternal DNA test that, in my bones, I knew would set the record straight. The results came back via email. I remember sitting at my desk, nervous to open the email, but I did, and there before me was the truth I couldn't wrap my mind, heart, or soul around. I wailed as if someone told me my dad had died— sobs so loud that my husband came rushing in to find me collapsed on my desk. He laid his body over me as a blanket of protection and comfort, allowing me to grieve from a place I never wish to visit again.

Unfortunately, the worst part was yet to come: I had to tell my dad. He, too, was convinced this was all a ruse. He had no doubt that I was his biological daughter—until I wasn't. I had to tell *my dad* that we aren't related. Just typing these words brings tears to my eyes. It was one of the worst days of my life.

For weeks, I couldn't look in the mirror. Suddenly, my own body no longer felt familiar to me. All the Hispanic was taken out of me—a sham of a costume I had worn for almost forty-seven years. I was embarrassed and heartbroken—the truth of who I really am still a mystery tied to details of someone else's story.

That's what messes do; they distort truth. They make you feel like you're out of control and there's no hope to ever control or change anything. So, you close the closet full of all your messes in hopes that no one will ever see them. You sweep them under the rug, because if you can't get rid of the mess, at least you can hide it! But eventually the closet hits its capacity to hold all the things, and the next time you try to open it, everything comes spilling out. You've swept so much under the rug that people start tripping over it.

Choosing Grief

We all have our own mess-coping mechanism. My go-to is eating popcorn with a ridiculous amount of butter and salt and watching all the Marvel and Star Wars movies. But this plan backfired this time around when the scene where Darth Vader says, "Luke, I am your father," did me dirty. But if closets, rugs, popcorn, and movies are off the table, what's left to choose?

We can choose to grieve.

I was taught that there are five, or maybe seven, stages of grief. In the most widely known and practiced model of grief, created by Dr. Elisabeth Kübler-Ross, there are five stages of grief: denial, anger, bartering, depression, and acceptance.[3] The five stages of grief are not meant to be experienced in a particular order but serve as a framework for the ultimate goal of acceptance.

While "there is little research to substantiate its validity,"[4] it's important to note that Dr. Kübler-Ross's grief model is "historically significant as it marked a cultural shift in the approach to conversations regarding death and dying."[5]

The Kübler-Ross model gave a framework of expected or anticipated behaviors when experiencing grief. Kübler-Ross's intentions were for this model to curate healthy conversations and give language to what is often a chaotic and traumatic experience. But in some circles, particularly the Church, its familiarity curated a rigid or formulaic way of experiencing grief. While this model brought awareness to the grieving process, with a concise and palatable understanding of grief, it offers limited help in knowing how to navigate grief or understanding the importance of doing so.

Remember the example of the kids who lost their father in chapter 2? They had a shared experience, but the words spoken to them at the time became the messages that guided their grieving process. This often occurs where grief and faith come together. Maybe you learned Kübler-Ross's stages of grief in church but were never given a clear understanding of the importance of navigating grief to our health.

Counselor Kay Bruner created an illustration of her perspective of how she frames the grieving process.[6]

Kay Bruner's Stages of Grief

Loss – hurt

Shock
Numbness
Denial
Emotional out
Anger
Fear
Searching
Disorganized
Panic

Loss adjustment

Helping others
Affirmation
Hope
New patterns
New strengths
New relationships
Re-entry troubles
Depression

Loneliness
Guilt   Isolation

Looking at this picture, one might assume that navigating grief means to strap yourself into the world's highest grief roller coaster and just panic and scream till you get to the other side. Although terrifying, at least the process is clear—you have to go down to get back up.

Or maybe you were taught the faith version of grief. I like to refer to this version as "cut-and-dry" grief, aka "Just pray about it," because that's what you do when you don't know what to do. Don't get me wrong, I believe in the power of prayer, but I also believe God gave us the gift of grieving. I love that Kay began with the first picture but then showed what the process of grief is really like.[7]

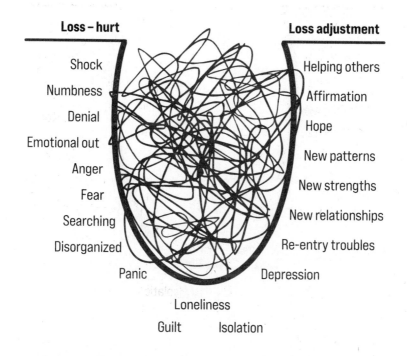

Loss – hurt   Loss adjustment

Shock   Helping others
Numbness   Affirmation
Denial   Hope
Emotional out   New patterns
Anger   New strengths
Fear   New relationships
Searching   Re-entry troubles
Disorganized
Panic   Depression
          Loneliness
    Guilt   Isolation

Sorry, kids, this isn't your average roller coaster. There's no straight up and down. When grieving, there are more twists and turns than you will know what to do with. This is the messy middle. Unfortunately, grief is often mislabeled as a "hot mess," when it should be labeled "grief in process."

I decided to take Kay's pictures and create a version of my process for my story.

Kay Bruner's Stages of Grief—Trish's Version

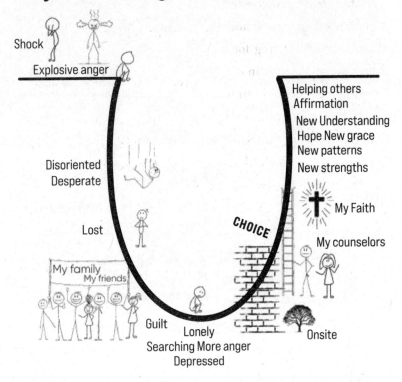

If my picture made you laugh a little, it's okay. As our daughter Janiyah says, "We laugh so we don't cry."

My mess started with a confession that led to shock, explosive anger, and anguish. I didn't read a book or ask for anyone's permission to feel this way. I was experiencing trauma, and those were my trauma responses that sent me free-falling into grief. The days and months that followed, I felt disoriented, desperate, and lost. Not only did I lose my dad and my identity in this process, but it all felt hopeless, which made me feel helpless—and helplessness convinces you that you are powerless.

In my hopelessness and helplessness, my hubby and my sweet kids took turns caring for me. My brother, Frankie, drove three hours just to look me in the eyes and tell me he loves me. Each of them in their own way sat with me while I sobbed one minute and spewed angry words the next.

But even with the support of my family, and my faith still intact, I felt stuck in my guilt for feeling anything and everything—which made me angrier, which created more guilt. I convinced myself I was stuck in a cycle of some kind of sadness insanity, with no way out. I needed someone to get me a closet or a rug, stat! I desperately wanted to get rid of this mess, or at least hide it. I just wanted it anywhere but in the middle of my life. I didn't want God to bless this mess. I wanted to go back to my life when I was still a Lopez, still Mexican, still 100 percent a part of my family.

The Power of *And*

What I couldn't see at the time is that grief and growth are not mutually exclusive. You can grieve and grow at the same time. In fact, sometimes grief is the biggest catalyst to your growth, if you learn to embrace it. God can use your grief to give you the motivation to choose to change. Your wounds may feel like they are sending you into a free-fall of grief, but the free-fall is grief choosing you before you have to choose it. Grief is sitting on the other side of the teeter-totter guiding you in your massive ups and downs to help you land softly and safely. Grief is a process of revelation, not destination. Grief reveals the power of *and*, meaning you can be ...

> Broken *and* hopeful.
> Wounded *and* healing.
> Angry *and* forgiving.
> Betrayed *and* chosen.
> Sad *and* joyful.
> Exhausted *and* expectant.
> Grieving *and* growing.

We see the power of *and* in Ecclesiastes 3:1–8 (NIV).

> There is a time for everything,
>   and a season for every activity under the heavens:
>   a time to be born and a time to die,
>   a time to plant and a time to uproot,
>   a time to kill and a time to heal,
>   a time to tear down and a time to build,
>   a time to weep and a time to laugh,
>   a time to mourn and a time to dance,
>   a time to scatter stones and a time to gather
>   them,
>   a time to embrace and a time to refrain from
>   embracing,
>   a time to search and a time to give up,
>   a time to keep and a time to throw away,

> a time to tear and a time to mend,
>
> a time to be silent and a time to speak,
>
> a time to love and a time to hate,
>
> a time for war and a time for peace.

The Tree of the Knowledge of Good and Evil is the choice of *and* and *nor*, not either-or. The apostle Paul knew this when he wrote, "For I am convinced that neither death nor life, neither angels nor demons, neither the present nor the future, nor any powers, neither height nor depth, nor anything else in all creation, will be able to separate us from the love of God that is in Christ Jesus our Lord" (Rom. 8:38–39 NIV).

You don't have to live in either the good or the bad; you get to live in the good *and* the bad, knowing that nothing—not your failed relationships, loss of identity, your regrets, nor even the tree full of a hot mess—can separate you from the love of God.

Grief understood in the *and* and *nor* allows grief to be your safe place to deal with your messes, rather than hiding them. Grieving is a choice to take a seat on the teeter-totter, laying your mess right in the middle. The choice to grieve may make you feel like you're stuck in a never-ending roller coaster of ups and downs, when really the teeter-totter of grief is moving you into deeper understanding, deeper healing, and a deeper capacity to accept the truth of your wounds without letting them get the final say.

The teeter-totter isn't where you're meant to live; it's a place to visit. God's love is wrapped in the gift of choice to embrace grief as a stopping point, not your final destination.

Acceptance isn't a stamp of approval to officially get over your grief. Acceptance is the acknowledgment of what was and what could've been. Acceptance is acknowledging your wounds and embracing the truth that grief is a process from which to learn and grow. Acceptance is choosing to live life to the fullest knowing there will be other hardships to overcome and other wins to be celebrated. Acceptance is believing that neither life nor death can take away being fully known and fully loved by God.

CYCLE-BREAKING PRAYER

Jesus, I come to you with an honest heart, asking for your help to embrace my grief and the ways it has been affecting my relationships. I know that grieving isn't a sign of a weak faith, but of one that is honest and vulnerable. I surrender this messy middle to you, trusting in your healing power. Help me process my grief through denial, anger, bargaining, depression, acceptance, and all the other stages of grief, in a healthy way that honors you and restores my connections with others. Guide me through this journey with your love and wisdom. In your name, amen.

4

YOU AREN'T AS STUCK AS YOU THINK YOU ARE

Justin Davis

We live in Indianapolis, Indiana. While we have moved several times over twenty-nine years of marriage, we have lived in the Indianapolis area the longest. It is home. Indianapolis is most known for the Indy 500, the Greatest Spectacle in Racing. I grew up about forty miles west of the Indianapolis Motor Speedway, and as I write this chapter, we live nine miles north of the racetrack, and yet, I have never been to the Indy 500. Just typing that makes me question my Indiana citizenship status.

Indianapolis is known for a few other things. If you are a foodie, you must know about St. Elmo's—the best steak house in Indy. Their shrimp cocktail is worth the trip and the cost. If you are a sports fan, we are known for the Indiana Pacers, the Indianapolis Colts, and, as of this year, Caitlin Clark and the Indiana Fever.

We are a loyal and troubled fan base. There is a cycle of dysfunction that accompanies being an Indiana sports fan. This cycle starts with stage one: the self-talk of a new season. You tell yourself you aren't going to get your hopes up. You aren't going to get emotionally connected to the team in any way. Your heart has been crushed in the past, and this year, you will not allow that to happen. If you keep your expectations low, then you won't be disappointed.

The next phase is overachievement. Because you haven't gotten your hopes up, the Colts and Pacers usually outperform your expectations. They win more games than projected. They overcome adversity and show grit and hard work. They lure you in throughout the season to make you believe there is hope. They win your heart.

The next phase is belief. You start to believe they will win. You realize that they will make the playoffs. They could win a playoff game. They could make a run. They could go all the way. Now, you're all in. You believe.

The last stage is devastation. They lose games they shouldn't lose. They melt down in the fourth quarter after having a big lead. Indiana sports teams are good enough to get you invested, but they only hurt you in the end. There is no book you can read to break that cycle. It's a pattern of insanity (sans the 2006 Colts Super Bowl victory) that I've been living in since the early 1980s.

Many people outside of Indianapolis don't know that our Children's Museum is one of the best in the country. The Children's Museum of Indianapolis, founded in 1925, is consistently ranked as one of the top children's museums in the United States. With over 482,000 square feet, it is the largest children's museum in the world and draws over a million visitors each year.[1]

When we adopted our youngest two kids, Jailyn and Janiyah, in 2017, they were nine and seven years old. The adoption agency and social worker we worked with helped us plan a few outings to help them get to know us and for us to spend time with them in fun and memorable environments. One of the first things we did with them was take them to the Children's Museum.

Trish and I hadn't visited the Children's Museum since our biological sons were younger, and one of the first exhibits that caught my attention was the new virtual reality experience.

This was in the early stages of virtual reality, before VR headsets like Meta Quest were released. I'd heard of virtual reality but had never experienced it. Once we got to the front of the line, we were given a headset with a long cord connected to a computer. It wasn't wireless like VR headsets are today.

On the museum floor, a line of masking tape stretched about fifteen to twenty feet. The objective was to put on the headset and walk along the tape to the other side of the VR area. It looked elementary.

First up was our daughter Janiyah. She was seven years old and had never been to the Children's Museum or experienced virtual reality. She put on the headset and immediately seemed like she was transported to another world. She started to inch across the floor with fear and caution. She said, "I don't think I can do this." I said, "Do what? You are walking on the floor." She said, "No, I'm not. I'm walking across a log, trying to get across a river." Every step she took was deliberate and slow. What should have taken about ten seconds in reality took her about two minutes in virtual reality.

Next was Jailyn. He was determined to do better than Janiyah. Within a few seconds of putting on the headset, he went from making fun of her for walking so slowly to being terrified of falling off the log and into the water. I reminded him that what he was experiencing wasn't real. "Jailyn, you are walking on a piece of tape," I said from the sidelines. He said, "If you saw what I am seeing, you would think differently." After a few minutes, he, too, made it across the "river" and onto "dry ground."

Then, it was my turn. I would show these kids how ridiculous they looked, inching themselves across a perfectly flat carpet along a straight piece of tape. I put on the VR headset, knowing my reality. I was on solid ground. I was secure on the flat floor. I only needed to walk a few feet to reach the other side of the room. But when my reality changed and became virtual, my mind was transported to a different reality. My movements were slow and exaggerated. I felt like I was one wrong step away from falling off the log. The water seemed real. The height of the log felt intimidating. What if I took the wrong step? What if my foot slipped off the log? How could I recover? When I got to the end of the tape, the worker at the museum said, "Go ahead and step down." Step down? How can I step down? I felt paralyzed. So, without even thinking about it, I raised my right leg waist-high to take a giant step down. Then, I raised my left leg and swung it around to lower myself off the log.

As I took off the VR headset and saw Trish and the kids laughing at me, I realized that my reality hadn't been theirs. They couldn't see what I saw. They didn't feel how I felt. Because of my reality, the height seemed higher. The step seemed steeper. It felt like I was one wrong choice, one bad step, away from falling off the log and into the water. From the outside looking in, I was terrified as I walked along a piece of tape on a flat floor at the Children's Museum. But my reality was drastically different. What was ordinary to those on the outside was intimidating to me as I experienced it.

As you seek to make choices to break cycles hurting your relationships and holding you back, no one can see what you see. You are the only one living in the reality of your situation.

Depending on how long you've lived in your broken marriage, financial situation, dysfunctional relationship with your parents, or codependent dating relationship, the choices that bring about change can feel overwhelming.

You might feel paralyzed because the stakes feel so high. Maybe you feel defeated because the hurt is so deep. The pain is so severe that you feel intimidated by all the choices you have to make to find healing.

The relationship seems too far gone. The marriage seems too distant. The debt is too massive. The abuse is too painful to heal. The cycle seems too hard to break. As you are reading these words, considering the choices that can change your relationships, you are thinking to yourself what Janiyah said to me: "I don't know if I can do this." Or what Jailyn said: "If you could see what I am seeing, you would think differently."

We talk to ourselves more than we talk to anyone else. The narrative we tell ourselves becomes the pattern of behavior we live out. Your internal voice tries to convince you that you can never change.

You'll never be forgiven.

You'll never overcome the addiction.

You'll always be a failure.

You'll never be married.

You'll always be lonely.

You'll never be loved.

You'll always struggle with bitterness.

You'll never fit in.

You'll always be a liar.

You'll never be good enough.

Decision Fatigue

According to a 2018 article in *Inc.* magazine, the average person makes thirty-five thousand decisions per day—what to eat for breakfast, what route to drive to work, where to go for lunch, what shirt to wear.[2]

The constant demand to make decisions leads us to what psychologists call *decision fatigue.* According to psychiatrist Dr. Lisa MacLean, decision fatigue is "the idea that after making many decisions, your ability to make more and more decisions over the course of a day becomes worse.... The more decisions you have to make, the more fatigue you develop and the more difficult it can become."[3]

In 2015, CNN.com profiled seven men as they recognized and tried to minimize decision fatigue. Among them were Apple CEO Steve Jobs, President of the United States Barack Obama, and Facebook founder Mark Zuckerberg. What each person had in common was their commitment to eliminate decisions in their daily wardrobe.[4] Steve Jobs consistently wore a black shirt, blue jeans, and

New Balance tennis shoes. President Obama wore only gray or blue suits. Mark Zuckerberg repeatedly wore a gray T-shirt and blue jeans.

In 2012, President Obama told *Vanity Fair,* "You'll see I wear only gray or blue suits. I'm trying to pare down my decisions. I don't want to make decisions about what I'm eating or wearing. Because I have too many other decisions to make."[5]

Zuckerberg said something similar in 2014. He told the audience of a public Q&A: "I really want to clear my life to make it so that I have to make as few decisions as possible about anything except how to best serve the community."[6]

If making decisions that bring change to our lives were so easy, we'd already have the changes we desire. We wouldn't lose our temper. We would be out of debt. We would forgive the person who wounded us. We could stop repeatedly arguing with our spouse about the same thing. We wouldn't struggle with the same sin repeatedly. Choosing to change sounds great, but when put in the context of all the other thirty-thousand-plus choices we make daily, it can feel tiresome and overwhelming.

You've probably heard more than once the answer to a common question when dealing with an overwhelming situation: "How do you eat an elephant? One bite at a time." Everything that seems daunting, overwhelming, or even impossible can be accomplished as you take one bite at a time. If you are the type of person who only focuses on the next bite, this is a powerful concept.

But what if you are the type of person who calculates every single bite of the elephant? Most elephants weigh between 8,000 and 15,000 pounds. Let's assume the elephant we will eat one bite at a time weighs 10,000 pounds. The average bite size for an easily consumable piece of meat is 0.5 ounces. Given those metrics, it would take approximately 320,000 bites to eat an elephant one bite at a time.

It's not the one bite that is discouraging; it's the 319,999 bites we know are required to heal a relationship or help us overcome what's holding us back. If change were as easy as one choice, we'd all have great marriages, thriving friendships, and loving relationships with family. We get defeated by the 300,000-plus decisions that seem necessary to change our reality.

In 2005, my sinful choices and destructive decisions placed our marriage in a place of overwhelming fragility. After ten years of marriage and three years after planting our first church, I confessed to Trisha that I was having an affair with her best friend. It was not a confession of remorse or repentance but of resignation.

Sometimes, the elephants we have to consume are because of our choices. That was certainly true for me. My choices placed me on the brink of divorce, co-parenting, and seeing my kids every other weekend. But Trisha had to deal with a 320,000-bite elephant that she didn't choose, didn't deserve, and had no idea how to overcome. What do you do when you are stuck in a cycle of someone else's decisions? By God's grace, we did the only thing we could do at that moment—we just took the first bite. We didn't try to figure out marriage restoration for the next year; we tried to do the next right thing that day.

What if I told you that you aren't as stuck as you think? As you confront your past, identify your wounds, and grieve what is broken, you begin to change your reality. One choice can break the cycle you are in and pave the way for the healing and transformation you desperately need, no matter how long you've been stuck.

In her book *Break the Cycle: A Guide to Healing Intergenerational Trauma*, Dr. Mariel Buqué said:

> Cycle breaking is how we put down that baggage of the past and step into a better future. Cycle breakers *choose* to be cycle breakers. It is an active, long-term decision. For you, that choice may have come after seeing the hurt that your family and communities have endured and no longer accepting that it must be passed down to the next generation. Or it could stem from your wish to create a different legacy for you and your lineage. One thing is for sure—cycle breakers across the world have one definitive goal in mind: to make sure that repeated generational patterns end with them.[7]

We all have baggage, and we all need a breakthrough. What I love about Dr. Buqué's definition of cycle breaking is that it's based in "an active, long-term decision." It's one choice to deal with our baggage and choose something different.

In John 5, Jesus encountered a man who had a lot of baggage and had spent years in the same cycle of behavior but not experienced any change.

> Afterward Jesus returned to Jerusalem for one of the Jewish holy days. Inside the city, near the Sheep Gate, was the pool of Bethesda, with five covered porches. Crowds of sick people—blind, lame, or

paralyzed—lay on the porches. One of the men lying there had been sick for thirty-eight years. When Jesus saw him and knew he had been ill for a long time, he asked him, "Would you like to get well?"

"I can't, sir," the sick man said, "for I have no one to put me into the pool when the water bubbles up. Someone else always gets there ahead of me."

Jesus told him, "Stand up, pick up your mat, and walk!"

Instantly, the man was healed! He rolled up his sleeping mat and began walking! But this miracle happened on the Sabbath, so the Jewish leaders objected. They said to the man who was cured, "You can't work on the Sabbath! The law doesn't allow you to carry that sleeping mat!"

But he replied, "The man who healed me told me, 'Pick up your mat and walk.'"

"Who said such a thing as that?" they demanded.

The man didn't know, for Jesus had disappeared into the crowd. But afterward Jesus found him in the Temple and told him, "Now you are well; so stop sinning, or something even worse may happen to you." Then the man went and told the Jewish leaders that it was Jesus who had healed him. (vv. 1–15)

The pool of Bethesda in Jerusalem was a place where sick people gathered with the hope of being cured of their disease. Bethesda in

Aramaic means "house of mercy" or "house of grace." The tradition for those with illness was to lounge under one of the five covered porches surrounding the pool, waiting for a miracle. They believed that an angel would descend and stir the water in the pool, and the first person into the pool after the divine touch would be healed.

As we read this today, it seems ridiculous that people would trust their health and future to something so outlandish. But as I look through my Instagram feed, I see frequent ads promising weight loss with no exercise, health "coaches" with no degree and minimal experience, and supplements to regrow hair on my bald head. We trust what gives us the quickest, easiest, or cheapest fix to our greatest need. These diseased people sat poolside day after day, hoping their change would come from winning a race with another sick person into the pool after the angel stirred the water.

The longer they sat looking at the pool, the longer they remained sick.

How We Process Wounds That Need Healing

If cycle breaking starts with how we deal with baggage, then let's examine how we process the wounds that need healing in our lives.

We Accumulate Them

We create some of the baggage we have in our lives. But some of our baggage is because of the choices made for us. You didn't choose your parents' divorce. You didn't decide to have a miscarriage. You didn't choose to be abused by a parent when you were a child. You didn't choose to have your spouse cheat on you. You didn't choose infertility. You didn't choose your baggage, but you have accumulated it.

In June 2009, my mom called to ask if she could spend the afternoon with me. Trish was out of town with the older two boys, and it was just me and Isaiah for the weekend. We had no plans, so I invited my mom to hang out at our house.

From the time she arrived, I knew something was off. I didn't know what was wrong, but she wasn't acting like herself. A few months before, my mom and dad had finalized their divorce after thirty-six years of marriage. My dad had a secret life of affairs and sexual addiction that came to light and ended their relationship. I knew how much my mom had been through, and at first, I attributed her demeanor to the pain she was navigating. But as she prepared to leave, she asked if we could sit down and talk. She had a bag with her and became very emotional. We both sat on the couch, and she took a Bible out of her bag.

She said, "The past few months have been some of the most difficult of my entire life. We have spent time encouraging your dad to be a man of truth, to be honest, and to live with integrity. The more I have gone after your dad to tell the truth, the more God has convicted me of my choices not to be a person of truth. One of the things God has laid on my heart is our relationship. I am going to tell you right now, Justin, that I am laying our relationship on the altar. I am willing to sacrifice our relationship to do what is right and to be a person of truth."

She continued, "You know that your dad and I married fifteen days after you were born. I got pregnant with you out of wedlock." I nodded. "What you don't know and what I have been lying to you about for the past thirty-six years is that when I met your dad, I was eight months pregnant with you. Your dad is not your real dad. Your dad adopted you when you were a toddler. He is your adoptive father, not your biological father."

My head started spinning. She could have told me I was from Mars, and it would have made more sense to me than what she was saying. I don't remember much of what else she said, but I remember asking her to leave. As soon as she was in the car, I called Trisha and told her about the bomb that had just been dropped on me. She couldn't make any more sense of it than I could.

If you are keeping score, two out of two of the authors of this book have found out their dads aren't their biological fathers. I found out in 2009 that my dad wasn't my dad; Trish found out in 2021. Sometimes, we don't do anything to create the baggage we acquire; it is placed on us. What we do with that baggage is our choice and our responsibility.

Look at John 5:5: "One of the men lying there had been sick [paralyzed] for thirty-eight years." We don't know the details of this man's life, but we can assume he didn't choose to be paralyzed. How we respond to the trauma and tragedies of our lives can determine the amount of baggage we accumulate. The people who sat at the pool of Bethesda didn't choose their illness, but they had to deal with it. Many decided to deal with it by sitting around other sick people every day, hoping to be first in the pool someday.

We Blame Others for Them

This man didn't seek Jesus out. Jesus saw him and approached him with a question: "Would you like to get well?" The man's response was surprising, given that he'd been paralyzed for thirty-eight years. "'I can't, sir,' the sick man said, 'for I have no one to put me into the pool when the water bubbles up. Someone else always gets there ahead of me'" (John 5:7).

When we live in destructive and dysfunctional cycles in our lives, it's easy to adopt a victim mentality. Jesus asked him a question that could change his entire life. "Do you want to get well?" The longer he sat at the pool of Bethesda, the more he blamed others for not helping him. No one cared about him. No one thought about him.

He didn't have anyone who would put him in the pool. People were inconsiderate of his condition, and someone always beat him to the pool and robbed him of his healing. He came to the pool at some point to find healing and instead had just accumulated resentment, anger, and a victim mentality. By that time, he was so buried in the cycle of his hurt that he couldn't ask Jesus for what he came to the pool to find—healing.

If you live with baggage long enough, becoming a victim is easy. Your temper is your dad's fault. Your broken marriage is your spouse's fault. The job you hate is your boss's fault. Your dysfunctional dating life is always the fault of the next person you date. The next chapter will discuss breaking the cycle of blame because it is central to healthy relationships.

We Settle for Them

> Inside the city, near the Sheep Gate, was the pool
> of Bethesda, with five covered porches. Crowds of
> sick people—blind, lame, or paralyzed—lay on the

porches. One of the men lying there had been sick
for thirty-eight years. (John 5:2–5)

As I read John's description of the pool of Bethesda, one question comes to mind: Had there always been five covered porches?
Did they start with one porch, and then, as more people came, they
had to add the covered porches to accommodate the crowds? Day
after day, week after week, crowds of people—blind, lame, and
sick—lay around the pool.

When this man first arrived, we can assume he had a lot of hope
for healing. Then, after a while, he resigned himself that change
was not probable. We don't know how long the man had been at
the pool, but we know he'd been paralyzed for thirty-eight years.
He became comfortable with his condition. He surrounded himself
with other people who had the same problems and just settled for
life on a mat next to the pool of Bethesda.

It is easy to get comfortable with dysfunction. We justify our
selfishness. We learn to live with and mask our insecurity. We get
used to struggling with our addiction. We become attached to the
anger that we've used to protect ourselves. If we can't experience
change, we can get better at being broken.

"Do you want to get well?" (John 5:6 NIV).

The question that Jesus asked the man at the pool of Bethesda is
the same question that he asks you today: Do you want to get well?
He doesn't ask if you want to feel better, offer to make the pain go
away, or offer an upgrade to a nicer mat. Do you want to get well?

I usually say yes to this question, but I want God to change my
circumstances more than heal my heart.

I want my financial situation to change. I don't want God to change how I manage my finances.

I want my marriage to change. I don't want to change how I treat my wife.

I want my kids to change. I don't want God to change how I talk to my kids.

I want my job to change. I don't want God to change how I view my job.

I want my relationships to change. I don't want to change my attitude toward difficult people.

Could it be that we are caught in dysfunctional cycles not because we don't want to change but because we have settled for behavior modification instead of heart transformation?

When our marriage imploded, and Trish was forced into a situation she didn't want or choose, she made one choice that changed everything. She packed everything I owned and kicked me out of the house. I wasn't broken, remorseful, or repentant. She made a choice not to enable my hurtful behavior. I would not change until the pain of staying the same became greater than the pain of change. That one choice brought tremendous pain, but it paved the way for healing and transformation.

As you read this, you may feel hopeless about overcoming what's holding you back. You feel defeated. You've tried to change. You've gone to counseling. You've read books and listened to podcasts, and things got better for a season until you ended up on the mat next to the pool of Bethesda. If you feel powerless or hopeless, I have good news for you. Jesus helps us when we've lost the ability to help ourselves.

In John 5:7, the sick man said, "I can't, sir, … for I have no one to put me into the pool when the water bubbles up. Someone else always gets there ahead of me."

God doesn't help those who help themselves. He helps the utterly helpless. As we surrender to Jesus' ability to heal, he does in us what we are powerless to do for ourselves.

What area of your life is lying on the mat? What area of your life have you lost hope that can be different? Your marriage? Your dating life? Your finances? Your relationship with an adult child? Your ability to overcome an addiction?

You don't have to have your life together or be a spiritual giant to be changed by Jesus. When asked by the religious elite who healed him, this man didn't know.

> But he replied, "The man who healed me told me, 'Pick up your mat and walk.'" "Who said such a thing as that?" they demanded. The man didn't know, for Jesus had disappeared into the crowd. (John 5:11–13)

This is the most incredible aspect of this encounter. Every miracle I can think of in the Gospels revolves around people seeking out Jesus. But this miracle, under the porch next to the pool of Bethesda, is one that Jesus sought out. This man wasn't a follower of Jesus. This man had never heard of Jesus. This man didn't recognize Jesus. Jesus didn't heal this man because of his faith. He healed him despite his lack of faith.

Everyone at the pool of Bethesda believed you had to be the first in the pool to find healing. This man couldn't walk. He had no one to help him. He had no chance of being first, ever. That is what religion looks like. The one who has their life most put together; the one with the best church attendance; the one who knows the most about God; the most educated; the most popular—those were the lucky ones in Jesus' day. Jesus went searching for those religion had rejected.

Jesus went to a man who had no chance of ever being healed in that system and brought healing to him. He was the most unlikely, the most overlooked, the man who had been sick for thirty-eight years and had lost all hope.

Maybe this describes you. You feel overlooked, unseen, disqualified, and like change isn't possible. You don't have to get your life together before you can find healing. It's just the opposite.

You aren't as stuck as you think you are. You don't have to make every choice required for change. Admitting you can't change is the first step in experiencing change. Another word for it is *surrender*. Jesus wants you to give up instead of trying harder. He wants you to come to the end of yourself so you can rely on his power to be made perfect in your weakness. He wants you to surrender. Surrender isn't defeat. Surrender isn't passive. Surrender is admitting you are powerless to do what you need the most: change.

Maybe you are thinking, *Justin, you don't know how broken my marriage is.* You're right, but God does. *Justin, you don't know how long I've struggled with anger toward my dad.* You're right, but God does. *Justin, you don't know how many times I've promised to change and haven't.* You're right, but God does.

Here are a few questions to consider as you contemplate the reasons you haven't been able to change:

What excuses are you making?

Who are you blaming?

What choice are you delaying?

Years ago, a counselor told me, "You can't heal a wound you don't give a name to." In the book's next section, Trish and I will help you identify and name the wounds holding you back. In each chapter, we will give you one choice you can make to experience heart transformation. This won't be a five-happy-hops to a better you. This will be soul-level work that you have to choose to find healing. But if you choose it, you can break the cycles holding you back and hurting the ones you love.

The change you desire isn't something God is dangling before you, hoping you can find it. He offers it daily with one question: "Do you want to get well?"

If the answer is yes, then your choice is simple. Keep reading.

CYCLE-BREAKING PRAYER

Jesus, I want to get well. I am tired of trying to overcome _____ on my own. I want to be healed. I can't overcome this on my own. I care about healing more than I care about pain avoidance. I am choosing to give this to you. Take it. Restore it. Redeem it. In Jesus' name, amen.

Part Two

NOTHING CHANGES

UNTIL

SOMETHING CHANGES

5

BREAK THE CYCLE OF BLAME

Justin Davis

I got arrested in my junior year of high school. Well, not officially arrested. Let me explain.

Growing up in Indiana, high school basketball was a big deal. I got cut from the basketball team in seventh and eighth grades. I made the team my freshman year and my sophomore year, splitting time between JV and varsity. In my junior year, I was not only a starter but one of our county's best players. My success on the basketball court went to my head. I loved the attention. I loved the popularity my basketball success was bringing. I started to think that the rules for other students didn't apply to me. I could show up late to school, turn homework in later than other students, leave school early on game days to go home, and nap before the game.

The school secretary was one of my teammates' mom, and she frequently facilitated my early game-day exits and afternoon naps. One Friday afternoon, before one of the biggest basketball games of our season, I went to the office with a few teammates to sign out and get a pass to leave school a few hours early. I was going to my house to hang out and relax for a few hours before returning to the gym for the JV game that preceded our game.

Three of my friends and I piled into my 1978 Datsun B210. It was a fantastic first car that cost $750.

The roads were snowy and slick, and at seventeen years old, I liked to drive fast regardless of the weather. Almost at my house, I approached a stoplight with several cars waiting for the green light. To avoid traffic, I turned to cut down a side street to take a shortcut to my house.

My quick maneuver and the icy road caused the car to keep going straight, and I smacked right into an old factory's concrete wall.

My heart was pounding, so I got out to assess the damage. I was fine, but my car was pretty banged up. Sure, the engine was still running, and at least one of my headlights worked, but the damage to the car's bumper and front right quarter panel was pretty nasty. Thankfully, I couldn't see any damage to the building other than a four- or five-foot streak of blue paint adding some newfound character to the brick wall.

My friends exited the car and immediately started making fun of me. I was shaking, partly because of the adrenaline of the accident, but mostly because I knew that my dad was going to kill me. This was 1990, so there were no cell phones. I started looking around to see where I could walk to call my dad and the police.

I started toward a house whose porch faced the street and was in full view of the brick wall my car had just hit. An older lady walked out on her porch. She said, "The roads are pretty slick, huh?"

I said, "Yes. I banged up my car pretty good. Can I use your phone to call the police?"

She said, "Honey, truckers scrape that wall all the time. You didn't do any damage. Go ahead and leave. No one cares about that wall."

So I hopped back in the car and continued driving to my house. I knew that my dad would be really upset, and I didn't want to deal with it before the game, so I drove my car into the garage, closed the door, and got a ride to the game with one of my friends. I thought I was in the clear.

A couple of hours before the game started, I was taking practice shots on the court when a police officer walked in. His son was on the team, so I didn't think anything was abnormal when he stepped onto the court in full uniform to talk to me.

Without any small talk, he walked toward me and asked me to stop shooting. Before I could even process what was happening, he placed my hands behind my back and said I was under arrest for a hit-and-run and leaving the scene of an accident.

This was only about thirty minutes before the JV started, so all eyes were on me as he walked me out of the gym. My face was red with embarrassment. The officer led me to his police car and drove me a few blocks downtown for questioning. I had never felt so terrified or so ashamed.

After about twenty awful minutes of making me feel like I would spend the rest of my life in prison, the officer broke the facade and told me about the setup. A second neighbor had seen the accident, wrote my license plate down, and called the police. My friend's police officer dad received the call, realized I was the culprit, and immediately called my dad. My dad found the busted car in the garage and then conspired with the officer to teach me a lesson. He had helped arrange this little interrogation downtown at the police station to scare me into never leaving the scene of an accident again.

When I walked out of the police station in my T-shirt and game shorts, my mom and dad were sitting in our van waiting for me. They were all smiles and started waving sarcastically. I was not happy. I refused to ride with them. Thankfully, it was a short walk from the police department to the high school.

I arrived back at the gym about halfway through the JV game. There was plenty of time to get dressed and physically ready to play, but mentally, I was out of it. I played horrible. I had one of my worst games of the season in one of our biggest rivalry games.

I was angry and humiliated after the game. I felt none of it was my fault.

The icy roads caused my car to crash. The only reason I left the scene of the accident was because the neighbor lady assured me there was no reason to call the police. I played horribly because the police interrogated me for thirty minutes before the game. My dad was at fault for losing the game and my worst performance of the season.

What I failed to take into account was the series of decisions I had made—turning quickly to avoid traffic, letting myself be talked out of calling the police, and delaying talking to my dad about the accident. But in my mind at the time, I was the victim of circumstances out of my control and choices others had made to sabotage my basketball game and reputation.

As long as I could be the victim, I could evade taking responsibility.

Looking back over the first thirty years of my life, I wish I could say that this incident was the only time I avoided responsibility and blamed others for my actions. But this was a pattern in my life by age seventeen, and it continued to be a pattern in my relationships with God, my family, and my friends. It almost destroyed my relationship with Trisha ten years into our marriage.

You may not have a father who orchestrated your pretend arrest for a hit-and-run accident when you were in high school, but there are probably mistakes you've made and sins you've committed and passed the blame onto someone else.

You blame your wife.

You blame your husband.

You blame your mother-in-law.

You blame your boss.

You blame your sibling.

You blame your kid's travel sports coach.

To experience authentic change and have healthy relationships, we have to break the cycle of blame.

What Is Blame?

Blame is defined as assigning responsibility for a fault or wrong.[1] In his book *Feeling Good: The New Mood Therapy*, cognitive behavioral therapist David Burns identified several cognitive distortions. Cognitive distortions are patterns of thinking that are false or inaccurate and have the potential to cause psychological distress.

One of the distortions that Burns addressed is personalization—the act of blaming ourselves for something that is not within our control. The flip side of this distortion is blaming other people for what happens in our lives. An example of this would be someone saying, "If the barista had made my coffee faster, I wouldn't have been late to my meeting."[2]

As Pastor Mike McClure Jr. said, "Responsibility searches for fault internally, while blame searches for fault externally."[3]

If you are a parent of more than one child, you know precisely what blame is. Let's say you have two children, a seven-year-old boy and a nine-year-old girl. You hear them arguing in the other room. Someone gets pushed into the wall, a picture falls, and the frame breaks. You go into the room to assess the situation.

Your daughter says, "He pushed me into the wall."

You tell your son, "You know you are not supposed to push your sister."

He says, "Well, she punched me first."

You say to your daughter, "Did you punch your brother?"

"Yes, but he called me a name."

You look back at your son. "Are we supposed to call names?"

He says, "No, but she took my hat and wouldn't give it back."

You look at your daughter and ask her if she took his hat. "Yes, but isn't he supposed to share? He didn't even want it until I put it on."

After this exchange, you break into an existential discourse on entitlement, gratitude, and how, when you were a child, you had nothing, and they should be thankful for everything they have because you can take it away at any time. (Or maybe that is just me with my blame-shifting kids.)

That is blame. Blame isn't just an unwillingness to take responsibility for our choices; it's assigning responsibility to someone else for our choices.

Why Do We Blame?

We are born with a predisposition to blame. No one teaches us to deflect. It's almost a reflex. It's almost natural. Our instinct to blame goes back to the very first human beings, Adam and Eve.

In Genesis 2, God created the heavens and the earth. Then, after he created everything, he looked at everything he had made and saw that it was good. Then, on the sixth day, he created Adam. But God said, "It's not good for man to be alone"; so he created woman.

Adam and Eve had a unique relationship with God. They were fully exposed before God, and they felt entirely comfortable. They were naked and not ashamed. They were fully known, and they felt fully loved.

God created this incredible home for Adam and Eve. He gave them everything they could ever need, and he gave them purpose, meaning, and his presence. Then he said, "You can have anything you want in the garden, but the one thing you can't have is the tree in the middle of the garden. Stay away from it, or you will die. It's not good for you."

But then, in Genesis 3, the serpent appeared and started to twist God's words, convincing Eve to question God's goodness. She started to believe that God was holding out on her and keeping her from all the fun.

> The woman was convinced. She saw that the tree was beautiful and its fruit looked delicious, and she wanted the wisdom it would give her. So she took some of the fruit and ate it. Then she gave some to her husband, who was with her, and he ate it, too. At that moment their eyes were opened, and they suddenly felt shame at their nakedness. So they sewed fig leaves together to cover themselves.
>
> When the cool evening breezes were blowing, the man and his wife heard the LORD God walking about in the garden. So they hid from the LORD God among the trees. Then the LORD God called to the man, "Where are you?"
>
> He replied, "I heard you walking in the garden, so I hid. I was afraid because I was naked."
>
> "Who told you that you were naked?" the LORD God asked. "Have you eaten from the tree whose fruit I commanded you not to eat?"
>
> The man replied, "It was the woman you gave me who gave me the fruit, and I ate it."
>
> Then the LORD God asked the woman, "What have you done?"
>
> "The serpent deceived me," she replied. "That's why I ate it." (Gen. 3:6–13)

How did Adam respond when confronted with his sin? He didn't take responsibility for going against the one thing God told him not to do. He didn't own his choice. He blamed God for creating the woman, and he blamed Eve for giving him the fruit. In one of the most efficient sentences in the entire Bible, Adam blamed God and Eve. He shifted the blame in seven words: "This woman you put here with me."

God then turned to Eve looking for an explanation: "What have you done?"

Eve responded, "The serpent deceived me."

When sin entered the world, so did the temptation to blame.

In a 2019 article entitled "It Wasn't My Fault," Dr. Ilona Jerabek and researcher Deborah Muoio analyzed data from 4,727 people who participated in a study on self-esteem. They compared two groups of people: those who readily admit mistakes and those who don't. Here are the five reasons they identified why people hate to admit their mistakes:

1. They "hate to feel low and weak."
2. They "tend to have deep-seated insecurities."
3. They "tend to have an extreme need for approval from others."
4. They "tend to be perfectionists."
5. They tend to "go on the offensive if someone points out their errors."[4]

Being confronted with a mistake is exposing. It's why hiding and blaming are in tandem in Genesis 3. When they were called out, rather than taking ownership, Adam blamed God and then blamed Eve. Eve blamed the serpent.

You Are a Victim

A victim is someone who's been harmed by another person's choices. Based on that definition, we are all victims to one degree or another. Maybe you were abandoned as a child. Your dad walked out on you, and you have no relationship with him to this day. Perhaps you were physically, emotionally, or sexually abused as a child. Maybe your parents got divorced when you were young, and you experienced intense verbal altercations that still affect you today. Maybe you've experienced betrayal by a spouse or ex-spouse. Maybe you were in an abusive dating relationship. Maybe you were homeless or in foster care growing up because of someone else's choices.

Your dad was an alcoholic.

Your mom didn't give you the love you deserved.

You were abused.

Your parents did get a divorce.

Your spouse did cheat on you.

Those are all real things. That happened. That was your experience. Those experiences will inform how you relate to God, how you relate to others, and how you see yourself. But those things, as painful, damaging, and heartbreaking as they are, don't have to define you or the choices you make in your relationships.

Earlier in the book, we talked about getting past our past because our past matters. Without healing from our past and the trauma and hurt we've experienced, we move beyond being a victim of a choice to the trap of victimization that begins to define our present and rob us of our future.

We are all impacted by other people's choices, but we don't have to allow their choices to define who we become and the choices we make. You were not able to choose what happened to you in the past, but you can choose to deal with it in a healthy or unhealthy way.

Dr. Alison Cook, in her book *I Shouldn't Feel This Way*, said, "When individuals blame shift, they put the blame on someone else for their problems instead of taking responsibility themselves.... What happened to you may not have been your fault, but your healing is your responsibility. Blame creates a cycle of victimization in our relationships that holds us back and keeps us from changing."[5]

The Trap of Victimization

Victimization is defined by Dictionary.com as "the act or fact of blaming others for the hardships one encounters in life."[6] Being a victim is something that happened to you. But when we start living in victimization, what happened to us becomes our identity.

Instead of seeing our experiences accurately, we process everything through the lens of what others have done to us. When we do that, we stop taking responsibility for our own choices. When victimization becomes our identity, we get trapped in harmful patterns, destructive relationships, and poor decisions. We often can't see a way out because we have become the one who receives from other people rather than a person who has agency and choices to determine our future.

In October 2005, I sat defiantly in a counselor's office on a Monday morning. The day before, I had confessed to Trish that I was having an affair with her best friend. It was a confession not of remorse or repentance but of resignation. She wasn't the wife I felt like I deserved, so I was done. Trying to save our marriage, a group of ladies at our church had made this counseling appointment for me. I went to the appointment to check it off my list before leaving my wife and three boys for the other woman.

I shared with the counselor the events of the previous day and my desire to start a new life without Trisha. She asked me about my faith, my pastoral and Christian leadership role, and whether I wanted to have a whole, healed relationship with God. She then asked me about the affair. How could I reconcile my relationship with Jesus and my choice to cheat on my wife?

Instead of admitting my sin and owning my destructive choices, I started to list all the things about my marriage that made me unhappy. I began to share with the counselor a narrative of my wife that I'd been writing in my heart for a few months. Everything was her fault. She was too critical of me. She was too angry. Nothing was ever good enough for her. I could never make her happy.

The counselor looked at me and said, "As long as someone else is responsible for your behavior, you will never change." Regardless of the truth about Trisha, waiting for Trish to change would only delay my transformation. The counselor wasn't concerned about changing my marriage at that moment. She wanted me to know that taking responsibility for my choices was the only thing that would save me from the trap of victimization.

Signs of Victimization

In his book *Abba's Child*, Brennan Manning said, "Whenever we place blame, we are looking for a scapegoat for a real dislocation in which we ourselves are implicated. Blame is a defensive substitute for an honest examination of life that seeks personal growth in failure and self-knowledge in mistakes."[7]

Victimization was a struggle for me growing up. I didn't know I was making the things I'd experienced and the wounds I'd accumulated a part of my identity until our marriage imploded. It took that crisis to wake me up to how I'd found my identity in being a victim.

In her book *Break the Cycle*, Dr. Mariel Buqué identifies sixteen examples of "Big T" trauma we can experience in life.[8] While it's not an exhaustive list, her premise is that experiencing one of these Big T traumas can cause us to create destructive cycles and damage our relationships.

Of the sixteen, I've experienced nine Big T traumas. Because I didn't understand trauma and wasn't aware of how these experiences affected me, I was victimized by them. I then made choices that victimized others in my life whom I loved and cared about. Blame became a defense mechanism for me to escape consequences and avoid responsibility.

How can you know if you are placing blame and living in victimization?

Disclaimers of Behavior

When we use a comma and add a *but* when we should use a period, we are doomed to repeat the cycle of blame.

I am sorry I hurt your feelings, *but* you shouldn't have said that.

I know I lied to you, *but* I didn't want to hurt you.

I know I said things I shouldn't have said, *but* my anger got the better of me.

I know I shut down during our intense conversation, *but* you know how I was raised.

I know I shouldn't look at pornography, *but* you aren't meeting my needs sexually.

I know I kept that purchase from you, *but* I didn't want you to be mad.

I know I was messaging that person on Facebook, *but* it wasn't a physical affair.

Trish and I do life coaching with couples and individuals from all over the country via Zoom. A few years ago, we were working with a couple in crisis because the husband had an emotional affair with a woman he met online. When his wife found out about the relationship and confronted him, he ended the relationship. The mistress then sent his wife screenshots of many of their explicit and inappropriate conversations. The reality of the affair was devastating, but the visual evidence was soul-crushing.

As we began working with them, we realized that their biggest obstacle to healing wasn't rebuilding trust, and it wasn't even repairing her shattered self-esteem. Their biggest obstacle was a statement he made in our first session together: "I don't know why she is so hurt; it wasn't even a physical relationship."

When we add a disclaimer to our choices, we minimize the damage our choices bring to our relationships, impair our growth, and set up a repeat of that behavior. We add a disclaimer to pacify the person we've wounded but have no desire to take full ownership so God can transform our hearts and heal the relationship.

Partial ownership is behavior modification, and eventually, the cycle will repeat itself.

Comparison to Others

It's never been easier to compare ourselves to others than it is today. Social media platforms, online forums, and minute-by-minute news updates expose us to others' faults daily. Public pastoral moral failure, Church abuse, and denominational cover-up schemes may still be surprising, but unfortunately, they are no longer as shocking.

Access to others' public failures allows us to view our choices, mistakes, and sins in comparison to others, rather than in light of God's standard.

In Matthew 7, Jesus said, "And why worry about a speck in your friend's eye when you have a log in your own? How can you think of saying to your friend, 'Let me help you get rid of that speck in your eye,' when you can't see past the log in your own eye? Hypocrite! First get rid of the log in your own eye; then you will see well enough to deal with the speck in your friend's eye" (vv. 3–5).

Focusing on the sin of others helps us feel better about ourselves. It allows us to justify our choices and come up with reasons why what we've chosen isn't as bad or as damaging as the choices of others.

I know I struggle with anger, but I'm not as resentful as she is.

I know my dating life is unhealthy, but at least I don't sleep around like he does.

I know we don't manage our money wisely, but at least we're not in as much debt as they are.

I know I value my job more than my family, but at least I don't travel as much as he does.

I know I shade the truth here and there, but I don't lie to my husband like she does.

When we avoid taking responsibility, we tend to judge ourselves by our intentions and others by their actions. Comparing ourselves to others will never bring the change we desire and will leave us in a cycle of blame.

The apostle Paul said:

> So why do you condemn another believer? Why do you look down on another believer? Remember, we will all stand before the judgment seat of God. For the Scriptures say,
>
> "'As surely as I live,' says the LORD,
> 'every knee will bend to me,
> and every tongue will declare allegiance to
>   God.'"
>
> Yes, each of us will give a personal account to God. (Rom. 14:10–12)

At the end of your life, you will not give an account for the choices of your parents. You will not be asked to account for the choices of your husband or wife. You will not give an account of your abuser. You and I are only responsible for our choices and decisions.

Pain Avoidance

In a message entitled "I Quit Blaming Others," Pastor Mike McClure Jr. said, "People who consistently blame others are not simply attempting to avoid responsibility; they are really attempting to avoid the discomfort and pain that comes with responsibility."[9]

Sitting in the counselor's office that Monday morning, pointing out my perception of Trisha's flaws felt less painful than identifying and addressing my own sinful choices. Blaming her was less painful than accepting blame. But that wasn't the first time I'd blamed her. It was the culmination of the victimization I'd been rehearsing in my mind for years. Focusing on her flaws spared me from the pain of facing the areas of my life I needed God to change and transform.

When we live in victimization, we adopt a posture of pain avoidance. If we can avoid pain in a relationship, we will feel like we're winning. But the destructive pain of repeated cycles is always more significant than the redemptive pain of taking responsibility for our choices. We prolong hurt and delay our healing by avoiding the pain of owning our mistakes.

Break the Cycle of Blame

I wish breaking the cycle of blame were a once-and-done choice that lasts a lifetime. The problem is that we continue to sin, be wounded, and inflict wounds on others. Breaking the cycle of blame is a continuous process we must repeatedly choose.

Here are some important steps as you commit to breaking the cycle of blame and embracing the healing that comes from owning your mistakes.

First, look for repeated patterns of behavior across all your relationships. It's probably not in just one relationship if you struggle with dishonesty. You may exaggerate details at work to make yourself look good. You may stretch the truth when talking to a friend. Adding untrue details to make a story better or more impressive seems harmless. If you are dating, you may withhold details about your past relationships that would negatively affect you. If you are married, do you hide things from your spouse that you believe would hurt the relationship?

Next, breaking the cycle of blame requires an honest assessment of your choices. This inventory can't be based on what was done to you in the past or the choices of any other person in your life. It can only be measured by your own choices.

What have I done that has damaged myself, others, or my relationship with God?

What have I said that has wounded others?

What have I pushed onto others for which I need to take responsibility?

Next, it's imperative to acknowledge how others have impacted your life and not blame them for your choices.

A few days after my initial counseling session, God began to break my heart for my marriage, and I started going to counseling. Trisha wasn't convinced I was committed to restoration, but she agreed to go to counseling with me a few weeks later.

As Trisha and I started the restoration process, the affair became an obvious pain point. How could we get over the devastation of infidelity? Early in our counseling journey, our counselor shared with us that the affair, while painful and destructive, was a symptom of much deeper issues in our marriage relationship. Unless we uncovered and took ownership of those, we would only repeat the dysfunctional patterns of the first ten years of marriage.

Thirty days into counseling, I confessed to Trisha that I was sexually abused as a child and had never told anyone about it, and I'd lived with the shame and guilt of that experience my entire life. I shared that I was addicted to pornography and had spent the first ten years of our marriage denying it and lying to her about it.

It was a defining moment, not just in my marriage but for me and my relationship with God. Was I going to blame my pornography addiction and affair on the sexual abuse I experienced? The abuse inflicted wounds on me that I didn't choose, and that was not my fault. How I pursued and found healing from that abuse was and is my responsibility. Sin (chosen or imposed) brings hurt to our souls. Not owning that sin allows us to live in a place of brokenness.

Don't skip over what others have done to impact your life, but make a decision to stop blaming them for your choices. It's painful, but life giving.

Finally, own your failures and bring them to Jesus. Maybe we don't experience the fullness of God's grace because we pretend we don't need it. Without ownership and responsibility for the sins we commit and the wounds we cause, we can't grasp and take in the scandalous, amazing, unconditional grace of Jesus. Realizing how much you need forgiveness places you in the perfect position to receive it.

Have you been battling, and struggling and wrestling, with the same issues over and over in your life, your marriage, your workplace? It's so much easier to blame someone else for the outcome of your choices.

When you are honest about your choices and you bring everything to Jesus, you are going to experience his grace, his mercy, his forgiveness. But this is why blaming others keeps you stuck, because as long as other people are at fault for what you've done, you will not bring it to Jesus.

These are my choices.

These are my mistakes.

These are my words that hurt.

These are the lies I've told.

This is my sexual brokenness.

This is my resentment that's destroyed relationships.

Owning our mistakes doesn't erase what happened to us by another's choice. It prevents what happened to us from holding us back and hurting those we love.

CYCLE-BREAKING PRAYER

Jesus, I come to you seeking your strength and wisdom to stop blaming others and living in a mindset of victimization. Help me own my choices and my failures. Give me the humility to recognize my part in the struggles I face. Give me the courage to take responsibility and the willingness to take steps toward healing. Transform my heart and lead me toward a life of transparency and growth. In Jesus' name, amen.

6

BREAK THE CYCLE OF UNFORGIVENESS

Trisha Davis

Nothing makes me go from zero to a hundred on the anger meter faster than driving in the car. I blame my childhood. Growing up in Joliet, Illinois, I attended Joliet Central High School, and my house was only 1.8 miles from the school. Technically, it should have only taken me seven minutes to get to school, but those 1.8 miles were like navigating through a maze.

GPS devices weren't available until 1992, and even then, your average teenager couldn't afford them. Google Maps didn't exist; not even Dora the Explorer and her trusty backpack were around to help me on my journey. Being a broke teenager in the '90s meant you had one option: a paper map.

To make my way to school, I had to go down a steep hill and cross a drawbridge—like the kind from the 1982 version of *Annie*. You never knew when the bridge would be up until you made it to the bottom of the hill. I always felt one of two feelings when I got there—elation that the drawbridge was down or rage that it was up.

Once over the bridge, I had to navigate downtown—which isn't that big, but it is made up of an insane amount of one-way streets. If traffic is bad, there is no turning down a side road, because you'd have to go the opposite way to try to go the right way. If I got stuck downtown, I knew I would be late to school.

Next up were the dreaded train tracks. Amtrak is a passenger train company that runs trains across the United States. Unfortunately for me, one of the passenger train routes started in downtown Joliet and went all the way to downtown Chicago. Like the bridge, you would either beat it or get beat by it.

Every morning, I was either believing in miracles when I made it through all those obstacles or raging and complaining why God hated me so much for allowing me to get stuck at every single turn. Through my fumes of anger, I would come up with the worst stories to tell the security guard at school so I wouldn't get written up for being late. By the time I got to the school, I had "killed off" most of my pets and family as my excuse for being late. Those 1.8 miles were the training ground where I became an expert in talking smack to people, bridges, streets, trains, and even God while driving in a car.

The Trap of Resentment

The journey toward resentment often starts on such 1.8-mile trips of anger. It's the little moments of frustration that seem unconnected until you wake up one day and realize all roads have led to a surprise destination. Upon arrival at this unintended stop, you're too tired from the journey to even care that the sign says, "Welcome to Resentmentville."

Breaking the cycle of resentment is like unwinding a ball of yarn to find the other end. Depending on your life experiences, your ball of yarn may be the size of a pea or the size of the moon. Regardless of the size of your resentment, the goal of this chapter is to understand how the thread of resentment grows from peas to moons—and how to untangle it from our heart.

Resentment, by definition, means "the feeling of displeasure or indignation at some act, remark, person, etc., regarded as causing injury or insult."[1]

Take a moment to slowly reread the definition.

At first glance, it seems on point, but upon closer inspection, it feels a bit suspect.

Consider how often you're on social media, checking the news, or encountering drivers distracted by their phones. Social media, in particular, has the potential to stir up displeasure or indignation in an instant, causing us to be triggered by a random remark or a subtle insult. By this definition, one might argue that we could all be living in a constant state of resentment. While I don't believe that's the case, it does highlight how quickly and easily our emotions can escalate, making the road to resentment easily accessible.

The Role of Forgiveness

The movie *Inside Out 2* is a hilarious and deeply moving animated story of a teenage girl named Riley navigating the onset of puberty. In the original movie, Riley's emotions as a child were guided by characters representing five main emotions—Joy, Sadness, Anger, Fear, and Disgust. But with the onset of puberty, five new characters join the party—Anxiety, Envy, Ennui, Embarrassment, and Nostalgia. A line of dialogue that sums up Riley's entrance into puberty is from Anger, who loudly declares, "Ever since that alarm [puberty] went off, nothing around here works!"[2]

The movie focuses so powerfully and beautifully on the role Anxiety plays in Riley's life. Spoiler alert: at the end of the movie, Riley has a full-on panic attack. As I sat with my family watching this scene unfold, the whole theater fell silent. We felt like we were with Riley, and not one of us knew how to help her get out of it. Silence was then broken by tears. We were overwhelmed by Riley's struggle with debilitating anxiety—a reminder to many of us of a shared experience you never want to share with anyone.

Then, the moment we all needed but didn't know we needed happened. Joy, the leader and most celebrated emotion, says to Anxiety, who is exacerbating Riley's anxiety attack, "You don't get to choose who Riley is. Anxiety, you need to let her go."[3] Joy's words were meant to elicit feelings not of joy but power—the power of choice.

Our emotions are conduits to process our experiences, but they don't get to choose who we become. We always have a choice—the choice to do nothing or to do something; the choice to feel and take healthy steps or the choice to feel nothing and do nothing. The choice is always there.

Resentment, much like anxiety, tries to take control and convinces you there's no choice to be made. Resentmentville is your permanent address. But just like anxiety doesn't get the final say, resentment doesn't get to determine how long you stay in your feelings of displeasure or indignation. You have the choice to leave. You have the choice to choose forgiveness.

For many of us, our understanding of forgiveness was shaped by our community and culture. Family, friends, teachers, coaches, neighbors—the list could go on and on. Our understanding of forgiveness is often shaped and formed by our experiences. Culture has taught us a lot about forgiveness through key catchphrases like, "Forgive and forget." "It's water under the bridge." "Let's put this behind us and move forward." And everyone's favorite, "Ask for forgiveness rather than permission."

Take a moment and try to think of a memory where you were marked by forgiveness. Is there a person or a moment in time that comes to mind? It could have been a moment when you received or offered forgiveness. The first memory that comes to my mind involves my dad.

As a third grader, I was invited to my classmate's birthday party. It was at the YMCA in the dead of winter, and this YMCA had an indoor pool! My dad took me to buy a gift, and when we got home, he started to wrap it. With as much third-grade sass as I could muster, I told him that I wanted to wrap it. I don't remember what the gift was, but I do remember it being odd shaped and difficult to wrap, but I was bent on doing it myself—and so I did.

My dad dropped me off at the YMCA, and after swimming, singing "Happy Birthday," and eating cake, it was time for presents.

My friend chose my gift first, and as she studied it, all the kids began to giggle at how goofy my wrapped gift looked. I hadn't planned for this outcome, so I even shocked myself when the words spilled out of my mouth: "My dad wrapped it." I threw my dad under the bad gift-wrapping bus, and immediately my stomach hurt. I felt so bad.

When my dad picked me up, I confessed my crime through dramatic tears, fully expecting him to excommunicate me from our family. I told him I was sorry for making fun of him in front of my friends. But through a smile, holding back his laughter, he told me it was okay. That's all he said: "It's okay." But what I heard was, "I forgive you." That moment marked me. Unknowingly, his words became my message that confession is good and forgiveness can easily be given and received.

Maybe your memory didn't end in a similarly positive manner. Perhaps your recollections involved pain, hurt, manipulation, or abuse. No matter if your memories are good, bad, or both, there's solidarity in our collective confusion about how to forgive. The insight that *Inside Out 2* provided about anxiety's role in our lives calls for an *Inside Out 3* to help us understand the role of forgiveness. Given the misconceptions about forgiveness, it's no wonder many struggle to give it or receive it.

Five Misconceptions about Forgiveness

While there may be a more exhaustive list somewhere out in the internetsphere, after twenty-five years of mentoring, pastoring, and coaching people, here are five misconceptions about forgiveness that I would put at the top of the list.

Misconception #1:
Forgiveness Equals Trust

Here are some of the misconceptions of trust and forgiveness:

- If I forgive someone, then I have to trust them.
- Trust is part of the forgiving process.
- If I don't trust them, then I really didn't forgive them.

But trust isn't a part of the forgiveness process. In fact, trust is a completely different part of the healing process altogether. While forgiveness is free, trust is earned.

Forgiveness is a choice you can make regardless of how the other person responds. You can forgive a person even if they don't receive it. You can forgive someone who is no longer alive. Forgiveness is a one-way street that can lead to the crossroad of trust—but trust isn't required.

Misconception #2:
Forgiveness Is a Onetime Deal

Some may think that the true measure of forgiveness lies in the ability to choose it just once. We make statements like: "Why can't I just forgive and forget?" "I thought I already forgave them, but I feel like I'm at square one again."

Wouldn't it be awesome if you only had to forgive one time? If you thought forgiveness was one and done, you are not alone. In Matthew 18:21, the disciple Peter asked Jesus, "Lord, how often should I forgive someone who sins against me? Seven times?"

This was kind of a comedic moment. Peter was going full-on teacher's pet, because he knew that in those days the Jewish rabbis taught you only had to forgive someone three times. *Only three times.* Imagine if we could go to a store, buy forgiveness stickers, and carry them with us to place on everyone we know we need to forgive. Forgiveness would be so easy. Three sticker strikes and they're out. Now, we wouldn't have any family or friends left, but at least the process of forgiveness would be clear.

Here's Jesus' response to Peter: "No, not seven times … but seventy times seven!" (Matt. 18:22). Simple enough, right? Jesus moved the number up a bit—to 490 times, to be exact. But Jesus wasn't giving Peter a mathematical equation; he was telling Peter that forgiveness is a process. Jesus knew that forgiveness is a process, not because a person needs to be repeatedly forgiven, but because of the complexities and layers involved in unraveling the pain caused by broken trust.

Misconception #3:
Sometimes It's Impossible to Forgive

When our marriage fell apart due to Justin's affair, reconciliation was made possible by navigating my way through the complex processes of forgiveness. For almost two decades, I have made it my mission to become an expert on forgiveness by being an expert forgiver. My expertise was made known when a publicist emailed me that Ed Stetzer, a well-known and respected leader and pastor within the Christian leadership community, had given them my name as someone who could discuss the topic of forgiveness.

I was so honored that Ed thought of me and trusted me to tell the world about the power of forgiveness through the lens of Jesus.

On August 31, 2015, I did just that. I went on Brooke Baldwin's show on CNN and told the world about the power of forgiveness.[4] This interview made it official—I was an expert on forgiveness.

I have shared my forgiveness story all over the country. Through blog posts, master classes, and global television, I have shared my story around the world—a story of forgiveness that has changed my marriage, my kids, and hopefully my children's children.

So why did I fail so miserably at forgiveness when my world fell apart ... again?

This time, it was due to an affair that happened forty-seven years ago. I thought I would know how to forgive. I thought I was prepared for anything that came my way. After all, I'm the CNN forgiveness expert. But my life was shattered in ways I didn't understand, and I didn't even know where to begin to pick up the pieces, let alone find my way to forgive. And in a bizarre twist that not even Hollywood could make up, Justin and I found out our dads weren't our dads in the same week (Justin for the second time). I don't know the statistics of that probability, but I know it has to be somewhere in the one-in-ten-billion range. Finding forgiveness was even more improbable.

Reconciling what you once believed as true with the actual truth can be disorienting and overwhelming, making it feel impossible to offer forgiveness for the deception.

I never once doubted my mom, really, in anything. My mom's teenage years were filled with so much tragedy and hardship. She didn't have the luxury of hiding the hard parts of her life.

When she was in the eighth grade her dad died of a heart attack, and then two years later, her mom died of cancer. My mom is one of five siblings. Her oldest brother was barely in his twenties and newly married when their mom died, and he didn't have the capacity to take all four of his siblings. Someone would have to stay at another relative's house. Although my mom could've gone with her twin sister, she willingly gave up going with her so that her younger sister could stay with her twin sister at their brother's house. My mom was a young teenager who had lost first her dad, then her mom, and now her siblings. What a tragic and heavy loss for a teenager to carry.

In the midst of her loss, my mom met my dad when they were in eighth grade. My dad is one of seven kids, which meant he had a lot of family to share with my mom. They dated off and on throughout high school, and then her senior year of high school, she got pregnant with my sister. She and my dad eventually married, and three years later, I was born. Eighteen months later came my brother. Even though my parents started our family at a young age, I never doubted their devotion to each other and us kids. In my mind, they were a love story meant for movies. My parents were my heroes, but especially my mom, because of what she had been through and the person she had become.

My parents were a power couple who created a beautiful family. And my perception of my parents was reiterated by my friends who often commented on how awesome my parents were—and they were right. They were a young, beautiful couple. My dad rocked the best hairstyles of the '80s and '90s. My mom was smart and gorgeous.

My mom was a legal secretary in Joliet for several years. She always looked cute and fancy when she went to work, and I admired her confidence. Eventually she found a job at a large law firm in downtown Chicago, which meant taking the train from Joliet to downtown Chicago, a forty-five-minute ride one way. She rode that train back and forth from Joliet to Chicago for thirty years! My dad didn't graduate from high school, but he became a known and trusted commercial painter. To say my parents were faithful and hardworking is an understatement.

Their parenting was no different. I was your typical high-maintenance middle child who was often complaining or crying about being left out—but never by my parents. As a middle child, birth order convinces you that life is not fair, but my mom and dad showed up to everything and anything I asked them to come to. In my mind, my parents were the couple who beat the odds. And my mom was the glue that held it all together.

When my parents divorced after twenty-five years of marriage, I was crushed, and my rose-colored view of my parents' marriage was shattered. It was a brutal season for our family. But it was especially hard on my relationship with my dad. I was mad at him and blamed him for their marriage falling apart. I had to reconcile what I believed to be true about my parents' marriage with the actual truth.

Their divorce rocked me to my core, and unknowingly, out of that pain, I began to create and operate out of unhealthy cycles in my relationship with Justin. If my "beat all the odds, rock star parents" couldn't make it work, how on earth could we? I tried to love Justin from a place of suspicion and labeled it "wisdom." My suspicions became true when our marriage fell apart years later.

But we did beat the odds. Justin and I did mend our marriage through repentance, brokenness, and yes, forgiveness. I had worked so hard to understand forgiveness through Justin's betrayal and his affair with my best friend. I thought I had become an expert in forgiveness. I mean, at least Ed Stetzer thought so, but this time, the betrayal from my mom seemed impossible to forgive.

It was an unfathomable betrayal. I couldn't reconcile in my mind that she would or could hold this secret from me—a secret she would have taken to her grave if I hadn't discovered the truth. I found myself being swallowed whole by another misconception many of us believe: This is impossible to forgive.

Maybe you've been there, where you've prayed through hot tears, "Jesus, you don't get it. You don't understand the pain of betrayal and disappointment. Why do I keep paying the price for other people's mistakes? I don't have it in me to forgive."

Jesus knew that forgiveness would be a daily struggle. In fact, in Matthew 6, Jesus told us how to pray daily.

> Therefore, you should pray like this: Our Father in heaven, your name be honored as holy. Your kingdom come. Your will be done on earth as it is in heaven. Give us today our daily bread. And forgive us our debts, as we also have forgiven our debtors. And do not bring us into temptation, but deliver us from the evil one. For if you forgive others their offenses, your heavenly Father will forgive you as well. But if you don't forgive others, your Father will not forgive your offenses. (vv. 9–15 CSB)

Jesus understood that just as daily bread sustains our physical bodies, forgiveness nourishes our mind and body in its own unique way.

Karen Swartz, MD, director of the Mood Disorders Adult Consultation Clinic at the Johns Hopkins Hospital, said: "'There is an enormous physical burden to being hurt and disappointed,' ... Chronic anger puts you into a fight-or-flight mode, which results in numerous changes in heart rate, blood pressure and immune response. Those changes, then, increase the risk of depression, heart disease and diabetes, among other conditions. Forgiveness, however, calms stress levels, leading to improved health."[5] Forgiveness calms stress—what an incredible revelation.

To be human is to be wounded, and to be human means to wound others. I wound people. You wound people. Romans 5:8 reminds us that the ground is level at the foot of the cross—while we were *still* sinners, Christ died for us. His choice to forgive us gives us the power to do the same. When we embrace the power of Jesus' forgiveness as a source of sustenance, rather than viewing it as an absurd or impossible task, forgiveness becomes an essential part of our healing process. The act of forgiveness doesn't excuse a person's behavior; it prevents their behavior from destroying your heart.

Misconception #4:
Not Everyone Deserves Your Forgiveness

We may need to sit with this one for a minute. Not everyone deserves my forgiveness. Wait, is that really a misconception? In Matthew 18:23–35, Jesus tells a parable about an unmerciful servant. It's a little lengthy but hang in there with me.

Therefore, the Kingdom of Heaven can be compared to a king who decided to bring his accounts up to date with servants who had borrowed money from him. In the process, one of his debtors was brought in who owed him millions of dollars. He couldn't pay, so his master ordered that he be sold—along with his wife, his children, and everything he owned—to pay the debt.

But the man fell down before his master and begged him, "Please, be patient with me, and I will pay it all." Then his master was filled with pity for him, and he released him and forgave his debt.

But when the man left the king, he went to a fellow servant who owed him a few thousand dollars. He grabbed him by the throat and demanded instant payment.

His fellow servant fell down before him and begged for a little more time. "Be patient with me, and I will pay it," he pleaded. But his creditor wouldn't wait. He had the man arrested and put in prison until the debt could be paid in full.

When some of the other servants saw this, they were very upset. They went to the king and told him everything that had happened. Then the king called in the man he had forgiven and said, "You evil servant! I forgave you that tremendous debt because you pleaded with me. Shouldn't you have mercy on your fellow servant, just as I had mercy on you?" Then the angry king sent the man to prison to be tortured until he had paid his entire debt.

That's what my heavenly Father will do to you
if you refuse to forgive your brothers and sisters
from your heart.

There are three scenarios at play here. First, the king offers forgiveness, only to have it manipulated by the person who received it. Second is the servant who was forgiven by the king and then refused to forgive his own servant. Lastly is the servant who asked for forgiveness, and his master refused. Who in this story do you relate to the most?

Maybe you've lived with the misconception that not everyone deserves your forgiveness.

The *CSB Study Bible* says this about the story:

> The ten thousand talents were equivalent to a billion days' worth of peasant wages. This was more money than was circulating in all of Palestine. In this story the king symbolizes God and to settle accounts symbolizes divine judgment. Thus, we see that in this allegory the sum represents the sinner's hopeless debt to God. Selling the debtor, his family, and possessions would hardly begin to recoup this debt. Forgiving such a loan is an astounding act of grace.[6]

The contrast shows that the sins of others against us are trivial in comparison to the enormity of our own sins against God.

"The word *jailers* literally means 'torturers.' The debtor's torture would continue until the debt was paid in full. Since the debt could not possibly be repaid, the torture symbolizes eternal punishment."[7]

Jesus told us to pray to God and ask him to "forgive us our sins, as we have forgiven those who sin against us" (Matt. 6:12). This is how we find perspective, rather than torture ourselves in the prison of bitterness and resentment. Jesus knew it would be hard, so he gave us a path to finding our way. Asking God for forgiveness helps us forgive others.

Colossians 3:13 says: "Make allowance for each other's faults, and forgive anyone who offends you. Remember, the Lord forgave you, so you must forgive others."

Misconception #5: Forgiveness Can Be Given Too Early or Too Late

Mother Emanuel Church was founded in 1816. It is one of the oldest black congregations in the South. This church was at the forefront of confronting slavery and was even burned in 1822 as a result. Since then, it has been a gathering place for civil rights movements, hosting leaders such as Booker T. Washington and Martin Luther King Jr. For many in the black community, Mother Emanuel Church is a beacon of hope and reconciliation.

On June 17, 2015, a twenty-one-year-old white male entered Emanuel African Methodist Episcopal Church, informally known as Mother Emanuel. He attended the church's Bible study for an entire hour before he opened fire on the others present, killing nine people, including the pastor. The shooter was a white supremacist who came with the intent to kill people of color. Only forty-eight hours after the tragic event, the victims' family members attended the bond hearing and were given the chance to speak to the shooter.

First to speak was Nadine Collier, who lost her mother, Ethel Lance. Her words are jaw dropping. She said: "I forgive you.... You took something really precious from me. I will never talk to her ever again. I will never be able to hold her again, but I forgive you and have mercy on your soul."

Bethane Middleton-Brown, the sister of Rev. DePayne Middleton-Doctor, said, "For me, I am a work in progress. And I acknowledge I am very angry." But she went on to say, "We have no room for hate, so we have to forgive. I pray God on your soul, and I also thank God that I will be around when your judgment day comes with him. May God bless you."

Anthony Thompson, the husband of slain Myra Thompson, fifty-nine, said, "I forgive you. But we would like you to take this opportunity to repent. Repent, confess, give your life to the one who matters most: Christ. So that he can change it, can change your ways no matter what happened to you, and you'll be OK. Do that and you'll be better off than what you are right now."

Their words make one wonder how they were able to offer forgiveness so soon, especially knowing it was only forty-eight hours since the tragic loss of their loved ones.

My friend Latasha Morrison, in her book *Be the Bridge: Pursuing God's Heart for Racial Reconciliation*, wrote this about the shooting and forgiveness: "Forgiveness releases us from the torment of our accusers and murders. It's not easy, but it's the only way into healing and wholeness: it's also a process and not something that should be demanded."[8] Everyone needs forgiveness, but it can't be demanded. The person doing the forgiving has to choose it on their own accord.

There's no timeline when it comes to forgiveness. Forgiveness can't be given too early or too late. Everyone progresses through the process of forgiveness at their pace. Not every family member of the nine victims was ready to offer forgiveness. Even after some of the family members offered forgiveness to the shooter, he wasn't remorseful. So why should the other family members even give forgiveness a second thought? Because, again, Jesus knows forgiveness doesn't excuse a person's behavior; it prevents their behavior from destroying your heart.

You might read that story and slip into believing all the misconceptions you've been taught. My friend, Jesus knows. Jesus logged a lot more than 1.8 miles with his closest friends and family. When he was in the garden, praying in agonizing pain from his impending death, he pleaded for his friends to pray as well, but they fell asleep. After he was tortured for hours and then had to carry his cross, the disciples were nowhere to be found to help. Peter, who seemed so interested in forgiveness in the past, had chosen to deny he even knew Jesus rather than help him.

Jesus knows what it's like to be disappointed and betrayed. Jesus knows—and wept and yelled and questioned "why" in the midst of being betrayed. Jesus shows us that forgiveness is only true forgiveness when we give it regardless of the person's response. Jesus taught us that forgiveness doesn't always restore relationships, but it will always heal your heart. When he rose three days later, he walked out of the grave and created a new road map to break the cycle of bitterness and resentment by choosing to forgive. He went first to help us go second, by leaving behind directions to navigate forgiveness in our 1.8 miles of daily wounds.

Forgiveness in the Messy Middle

Ephesians 4:32 says, "Be kind to one another, tenderhearted, forgiving one another, as God in Christ forgave you" (ESV).

Forgiveness is what has kept me softhearted and helped me see beyond my rose-colored lenses to see my hurts and the people who have caused them from a thirty-thousand-foot perspective. Pursuing forgiveness in the messy middle has given me an aerial view of the whole person by acknowledging their life obstacles.

My relationship with my mom isn't what it was, but it is on the mend. We are choosing 1.8 miles of restoration at a time. And while offering forgiveness doesn't excuse the hurt her choices have caused me, forgiveness helps me not to reduce her to the sum of her choices. Because at the end of the day, the ground is level at the foot of the cross. My need for forgiveness from God far exceeds the forgiveness I need to extend to my mom.

So, it turns out I'm not a forgiveness expert, after all, and that's okay, because forgiveness wasn't meant to be mastered; it was meant to be given and received—a gift given by our Savior to navigate our way back to him and sometimes each other. Although forgiveness may not restore our relationships, it will always resurrect the parts of our heart bitterness tries to destroy. Forgiveness isn't the finish line but the starting line to the road of healing.

CYCLE-BREAKING PRAYER

Jesus, I come to you seeking your help to acknowledge the resentment in my heart. I know I can't break the cycle of bitterness until I admit it to you. Help me understand the depth of your forgiveness so that I can extend that same forgiveness to those I'm withholding it from. Give me the strength to let go, so I can find the freedom and healing that come from living in your grace. Transform my heart and fill it with your love. In your name, amen.

7

BREAK THE CYCLE OF FEAR

Trisha Davis

Justin and I have taken our kids to Florida for spring break since they were toddlers. It was often our only vacation for the year, so we all looked forward to a week of fun in the sand and sun. Over the years, we mastered finding great condos on the beach through a company that always has the best and most affordable places to stay. But spring break 2019 was *extra* in all the wrong ways.

I found an incredible three-bedroom condo with panoramic views from the living room and primary bedroom. It was the first time I had found a three-bedroom on the beach in our price point. I was pumped, because it meant I could invite all my people on spring break. First, I invited my mother-in-law, who had never gone on vacation for spring break. Next, I asked our oldest son, Micah, and his wife, Rylei. It was going to be the best time away. I was giddy.

Three years prior to this spring break, we had planted a church, adopted our son and daughter, sent another kid to college, and married off our firstborn. Our house was a revolving door of transition, and I was desperate for something that felt familiar and grounding. Spring break was exactly what I needed.

As we left our home in Indiana and started down Interstate 65, I felt the stress melt away. Even though we were still hundreds of miles away, I could smell a hint of the sea salt air. Several hours later, that smell became real. When we arrived, I swung open the car door and took in the deepest breath. But mid-exhale, I noticed something was amiss. That beautiful view I had been looking forward to was blocked by a huge structure being built next door. All we could see were steel and concrete.

It's fine, I thought to myself. It was disappointing, for sure, but the beach was still in our view if we just looked straight ahead. I inhaled the salty air once again and exhaled my frustration as our crew headed toward our condo. I dramatically opened the door and said, "Welcome to my casa on the beach, everyone." But as we stepped inside, the fresh air was replaced with the fresh scent of mold and a hint of garbage—and it just went downhill from there.

Walking through the condo, we noticed things you never want to see in your vacation home—or any home for that matter. The refrigerator had bugs. The bed covers throughout the condo had stains straight out of a *Law & Order* episode. The tile on the floor was no longer attached, and the "TV" was a makeshift computer monitor screen hooked up to bunny ears. The outdoor furniture was so rusted that just being near it warranted a tetanus shot. And to add insult to injury, it rained and rained, and rained, and rained, and rained every single day. And like the Wicked Witch of the West, this girl was melting.

My dream vacation was turning into a nightmare, and it hadn't even started. We woke up every morning not to the sounds of soothing ocean waves but to a myriad of workers using nail guns, hammers, and saws. I found myself taking it out on my innocent husband, like a two-year-old who couldn't or wouldn't stop whining and having emotional outbursts. Even though Justin had nothing to do with the house being built next door, the bugs, the stains, the broken floor tiles, or the rain, I was relentless in my laments. My lament went something like, "I just need a break! Why can't I have quality time with my people? This is going to be our only time away!"

I was a mess. I was so stressed about what would happen to my family and me if this vacation didn't go as planned, because I knew we all needed it. I was convinced that if we didn't have this time away as a family, I would fall apart, my marriage would unravel, and my family wouldn't be able to move on as healthy human beings.

At first glance, this story seems all about exhaustion, transition, and burnout, which are all valid and somewhat true assumptions. But those weren't my drivers. I was being driven by fear—of not getting rest, of going home more stressed than when I came, of my relationships crumbling. Fear was driving my heart, mind, and soul.

The fear of this vacation failing paralyzed me, and in my fear, I made great friends with bitterness. This vacation was miserable due in part to the circumstances but more so because my fear of it failing made misery my mission. Fear was the neighbor's house blocking not only my view of the ocean but my ability in the moment to see that one vacation would not make or break me or my family.

Defining Fear

Fear mishandled robs us of truth and perspective. Fear misunderstood keeps us stuck in cycles of bitterness, defensiveness, defeatism, and isolation. Fear creates more chaos in an already chaotic heart and mind. *The Holman Illustrated Bible Dictionary* says fear is a:

> Natural emotional response to a perceived threat to one's security or general welfare. It ranges in degree of intensity from a sense of anxiety or worry to one of utter terror. It can be a useful emotion when it leads to appropriate caution or measures that would guard one's welfare. On the other hand, fear can be a hindrance to the enjoyment of life if it is induced by delusion or if it lingers and overpowers other more positive emotions such as love and joy, perhaps leading to an inability to engage in the normal activities of life. In the Bible, however, fear is perhaps more often than in popular culture regarded not as pure emotion but as wise behavior.[1]

The truths within this definition of fear are astounding. Against the backdrop of my vexed vacation, I pretty much hit every type of fear response possible. The perplexity of fear is often reduced to a singular purpose or meaning, indicating that fear is bad and that being fearless is good. But the problem with being fearless is that it means removing fear altogether. It's all or nothing.

But what if fear is a guide, not a barrier, to fearlessness? What if fear is the very emotion that breaks through the chaos of what is or what could be to leave us with the power of choice? The choice is to let fear paralyze you or empower you. Think about the times you were most fearful. How often was there a decision that needed to be made attached to that fear?

A new job opportunity opened, but you feared taking it because you were uncertain how you would fit in the new role—so you chose to pass it up.

An unexpected friendship begins with the new family that moved in next door, but you fear the fallout that might affect your relationship—so you choose not to befriend them.

You finally get out of debt, and a once-in-a-lifetime opportunity to go abroad arises. Even though you can afford it, fear of potential financial problems keeps you from going.

You know you're overextended in every area of life, but the fear of missing out keeps you saying yes to people and opportunities that deplete you.

The aftermath of fear-informed choices is often shame, embarrassment, and defeat. We shame ourselves for feeling fear to begin with. Our self-talk turns into thoughts such as:

- "If I were just brave enough, I could've interviewed and maybe landed that new job."

- "If I had overcome my fear of failed relationships, I could have had a community I so desperately needed."
- "I'm never going to get over my fear of _____, so why even try?"

Our fear gets pinned against our desires, and when fear wins, we settle for the black eye of shame, embarrassment, and defeat.

Fear is the most difficult cycle to quantify, unlike most of the cycles we have discussed. There are different intensities of fear, different aspects of fear, and a myriad of definitions of fear. Our fears are often not even quantified as fear.

In his book *Mastering Fear: Harnessing Emotion to Achieve Excellence in Work, Health, and Relationships*, Robert Maurer took a clinical and psychological approach to understanding fear. While this book is not faith-based, it's one of the best books I've ever read about fear. It starts with the premise that, as kids, we embrace fear as a part of life:

> By the time we become adults, however, fear is no longer seen by most of us as a normal, healthy part of life, but instead something we get angry at for showing up. In a culture obsessed with self-reliance and the preservation of self-esteem, the term *fear* has become a four-letter word. We do not accept our lack of control and so we rarely learn how to deal with it successfully.[2]

"We do not accept our lack of control." [Insert Macaulay Culkin picture with hands on face here.]

For many of us, fear is equated with a lack of control. But fear isn't a lack of control; quite the opposite. Fear guides us to the core of our unspoken expectations, dreams, hurts, and beliefs. Fear awakens our body to feel our thoughts, not just think them. Fear brings forth a full-body, all-in, take-me-to-the-cliff's-edge choice.

What if we began to flip the script and look at fear as the starting point to wisdom? What if the fear you are struggling with the most became the catalyst for the change you desire?

What if fear is steering you to a choice rather than a dead end?

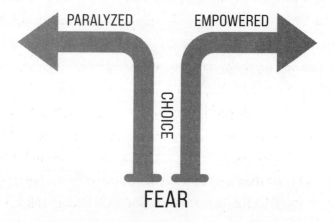

PARALYZED   EMPOWERED

CHOICE

FEAR

A viral video sparked a trend where people, while sitting in a car with someone, suddenly scream as loud as they can for no apparent reason. This not only startles the other person but often makes them scream as well. What makes the videos so hilarious are the responses. When one person starts screaming, the other starts screaming too, although they have no idea why they are screaming.

Fear Demands a Response

Our initial reaction to fear is our fight-or-flight response. It's the light switch, the initial knee-jerk reaction we have no control over; there's no time to think; just do. Just ask my kids how many times I have whacked them across their chests to "protect" them when slamming on the brakes in the car. The initial response to fear is unavoidable, but when the shock of what happened wears off, we have the free agency of choice.

The amygdala is "a ganglion of the limbic system adjoining the temporal lobe of the brain and involved in emotions of fear and aggression."[3] In laypeople's terms, it plays a massive role in our reaction to fear. Knowing and understanding this little almond-shaped part of your brain is important because it's the switch that gets flipped to turn on your whole body. When you have a fear response, you're not being good or bad, just as fear isn't good or bad. Your amygdala is the neon sign that starts flashing "DANGER."

I have spent the past three decades sitting with people in their pain. Whether as a mentor, ordained pastor, or life coach, I have sat with students, young adults, retirees, and everybody in between. And no matter their age or season of life, everyone has experienced some form of broken trust. *Trust* is our safety word. Think about jumping off a cliff tethered to a bungee cord. The only question you have in that moment is, "Can this cord be trusted?" So, it's understandable that we experience worry, anxiety, fear of the unknown, and guardedness when it comes to trusting people.

In my own stories of broken trust, I know what it's like to wrestle with fear. I have a strange history of broken trust in my relationships. Every season of my life, from birth to junior high to adulthood, I've had a significant woman in my life betray my trust. Many of the stories I didn't learn about until I was an adult, but each time the truth came out, I had to make a choice: I could let fear rob me of female friendships or choose risk, wisdom, grace, and understanding.

The point of sharing this part of my life isn't for pity but rather to emphasize that I am an expert on betrayal trauma, forged through my own stories. I know what it's like to sit at the cliff's edge of fear and choose the familiarity of living paralyzed. But familiarity always tricks us into equating it with safety. You know you are living for the familiar when you do the same things over and over again and expect different results—which is the definition of *insanity*, not safety.

I want to invite you to choose something different with your fear. I want you to stand at the cliff's edge of fear and see a different choice—the choice to be empowered through risk, grace, new understanding, and wisdom.

The book of Job is the most exhausting book in the Bible to read. Give me Leviticus over Job any day of the week. Job's story is soul-crushing. He was a man who had it all—a great faith, a great family, and great wealth. But the book of Job begins with a bizarre conversation between God and Satan.

This conversation took place in heaven. "One day the angels came to present themselves before the LORD, and Satan also came with them. The LORD said to Satan, 'Where have you come from?'" (Job 1:6–7 NIV).

I have so many thoughts and questions about God's response, but let's stay on the topic at hand. Right out of the gate, their conversation went sideways.

Satan answered the LORD and said, "From going to and fro on the earth, and from walking up and down on it." And the LORD said to Satan, "Have you considered my servant Job, that there is none like him on the earth, a blameless and upright man, who fears God and turns away from evil?" Then Satan answered the LORD and said, "Does Job fear God for no reason? Have you not put a hedge around him and his house and all that he has, on every side? You have blessed the work of his hands, and his possessions have increased in the land. But stretch out your hand and touch all that he has, and he will curse you to your face." (Job 1:7–11 ESV)

While God is all-knowing, Satan is not. God knew how Job's story would end, and yet Satan was desperate to prove God wrong about humanity. He has made it his mission to roam the earth, collecting stories of humanity's failures and using them to accuse God of his. He does this by repeatedly using the same tactic—posing fear-induced questions, *even to God*.

We see this tactic used for the first time in the garden of Eden, where Satan asked Eve, "Did God really say, 'You must not eat from any tree in the garden?'" Satan did nothing to physically make Eve eat the fruit from the Tree of the Knowledge of Good and Evil. He just posed a question. He then followed with an accusatory statement: "'You won't die!' the serpent replied to the woman. 'God knows that your eyes will be opened as soon as you eat it, and you will be like God, knowing both good and evil'" (Gen. 3:4–5).

Satan accused God of holding out on her and said that if she would just eat the fruit from the forbidden tree, she would be as wise as God. We understand Eve's state of mind because verse 6 says that the fruit was pleasing to her eyes, and she believed Satan's lie that it would give her wisdom God wouldn't provide.

Satan used the same tactic in his conversation with God. It is mind-blowing that, even standing in the presence of God and all his glory, Satan believed he could beat God through human failure. But God had Job.

"Have you noticed my servant Job? He is the finest man in all the earth. He is blameless—a man of complete integrity. He fears God and stays away from evil" (Job 1:8). Job was highly respected (Job 29:7–11), a fair and honest judge (29:7, 12–17), a wise counselor (29:21–24), an honest employer (31:13–15, 38–39), hospitable and generous.[4] He was God's ace in the hole to display what faith and friendship between him and humanity looked like.

Satan (which means "adversary" or "accuser" in Hebrew) wasn't fazed. He began to accuse God with cunning questions: "Satan replied to the LORD, 'Yes, but Job has good reason to fear God. You have always put a wall of protection around him and his home and his property. You have made him prosper in everything he does. Look how rich he is! But reach out and take away everything he has, and he will surely curse you to your face!'" (Job 1:9–11).

Satan accused God of giving Job a perfect life, asserting that's why he feared God and was so perfect. Take away everything precious to Job, and just like Anakin Skywalker, watch him turn to the Dark Side of the Force. So begins the story of Job losing every-thing—his wife, children, and extended family. He lost his wealth and health. Job lost everything.

Throughout *thirty-seven* chapters, Job lamented, and the reader's heart breaks for the plight that became his life. A few short chapters in, friends got involved, and at first, they made space for him and sat with him in his pain. But a short time after, Job's three friends— Eliphaz, Bildad, and Zophar—got "exhausted" from listening to Job's laments. Eventually, their advice turned to accusations, which brought Job to his breaking point.

Here are just a few of Job's responses:

"Don't I have a right to complain?" (Job 6:5).

"One should be kind to a fainting friend, but you accuse me without any fear of the Almighty" (Job 6:14).

"You, too, have given no help. You have seen my calamity, and you are afraid" (Job 6:21).

"I cannot keep from speaking. I must express my anguish. My bitter soul must complain" (Job 7:11).

"I am disgusted with my life. Let me complain freely. My bitter soul must complain" (Job 10:1).

"It is a land as dark as midnight, a land of gloom and confusion, where even the light is dark as midnight" (Job 10:22).

Job wasn't trying to fake it until he made it. There was no "I'm fine" in his vocabulary; he was fully transparent about his pain. He felt confused, bitter, and in a dark place. Fear is mentioned in two ways. In verse 6:14, *fear* is meant as reverence of God. In verse 21, the word *afraid* in Hebrew means something more intense, like "terrified."

It is argued that, despite the difference in terminology, the "fear of God" is equivalent to the "fear of the LORD" concept of Proverbs. The location of the motif in the final form of the book of Job suggests that the "fear of God" is not being proposed as the answer to Job's dilemma. Rather, Job maintains his "fear of God" throughout the book but is left with questions and suffering. The "fear of God" is seen as the solution by Job's friends, the wisdom interlude of chapter 28, and by Elihu, yet all this is overridden by the Yahweh speeches and epilogue, where the "fear of God" is not mentioned. While the "fear of God" is central to the wisdom stream, the book of Job establishes that it is not the answer to every problem in life.[5]

The story of Job starts with Satan posing fear-induced questions to God followed by an accusation. We see him using the same tactic with Job through his friends. We see him use this same tactic with Jesus in the wilderness, where he gives the fear-induced challenge, "If you are the Son of God, tell these stones to become loaves of bread" (Matt. 4:3). This is followed by an accusation using Scripture: "For he will order his angels to protect you wherever you go. They will hold you up with their hands so you won't even hurt your foot on a stone" (Ps. 91:11–12). Satan's goal is to use fear as the bait to keep you stuck in fear, with the hopes you will stay there.

The fear-induced question being spoken over us today is, "Didn't God really say fear would keep you safe?" And the accusation is,

"Doesn't Scripture say the fear of the Lord is your strength?" Satan's goal is to deceive with lies that appear as truth—lies that distort truth and skew perspectives.

Unhealthy Response to Fear

In his book *Mastering Fear*, Robert Maurer used the mnemonic "DANGERS" to explain the unhealthy ways we can respond to fear, responses where our fears distort truth and skew perspectives.

Depression
Anger
Negotiations
Griping
Eating
Rumination
Substances[6]

While I won't unpack every word, three words stand out to me: depression, griping, and rumination. Maurer said this about depression:

Although there is much about depression that remains a mystery, there is some evidence supporting the idea that depression may be one result of long-term activation of the amygdala; and certain mild depression may mask underlying fear.[7]

As someone who has battled with depression, this correlation wasn't a surprise. Feeling stuck by paralyzing fear brings frustration and often leads to a deep sadness over the belief that there's no way out.

Sadness + A Long Period of Time = Stuck in Fear.

As soon as I started reading Maurer's section on griping, I knew I was in trouble. Remember my story about my major vacation meltdown? The author could have used me as an example to describe griping. In essence, he explained that griping happens when lots of change and transition take place in a person's life:

> Individuals can become very negative, complaining loudly and in-depth as they struggle with uncertainty (another "grown-up" word for fear) in the workplace, community, at home, or even in their own bodies as they age or as health concerns arise.[8]

Ouch.

When I read this for the first time, I found Justin sitting in the living room and said, "BABE! I have got to read this to you." I read the entire section to him both in laughter, confession, and validation. The loud and in-depth complaining part made me belly laugh. But in all seriousness, if someone would have called me out on my behavior during vacation (oh, wait, Justin did), I wouldn't have believed my griping was out of fear.

Transition + Uncertainty = Stuck in Fear.

Lastly, the author explained the word *rumination* in a palatable way. Rumination is "worry without resolution. Rather than calming our fears, we ruminate on them."[9] I would define rumination as "bed brain." You know, the thoughts you can't shut off in your brain as you lie in bed. You just ruminate over the same situation over and over again, knowing you have no way of resolving the situation.

Ruminating + No Resolution = Stuck in Fear.

Our danger responses to fear keep us stuck in the cycle of distorted truth and skewed perspectives. But rather than seeing fear as bad, we can actually make fear our ally. Fear can guide us to the edge to see that there is another choice other than being stuck in paralyzing fear. Fear can be a catalyst for empowerment.

As much as Satan wants to throw shade with his fear-induced questions, *fear doesn't get to choose.* Yes, we have our amygdalas that provide our first response to fear, but that's not the end of the story. Fear doesn't get the final say. You get to choose, like Job. He was still fatigued from his physical and emotional journey. Job was depressed, griping at God and his friends, and at the end of himself—yet he didn't sin. He allowed his fear to guide him to the edge of himself, and instead of being paralyzed, he found empowerment through God's grace, understanding, and wisdom:

> God alone understands the way to wisdom;
>   he knows where it can be found,
> for he looks throughout the whole earth
>   and sees everything under the heavens.
> He decided how hard the winds should blow
>   and how much rain should fall.
> He made the laws for the rain
>   and laid out a path for the lightning.

Then he saw wisdom and evaluated it.

He set it in place and examined it thoroughly.

And this is what he says to all humanity:

"The fear of the Lord is true wisdom;

to forsake evil is real understanding."

(Job 28:23–28)

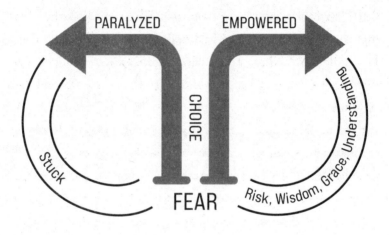

You Are Safe with God

We see this again and again in the life of Jesus. Before Jesus started his public ministry, God told him to go out into the wilderness alone and fast for forty days and forty nights. On the last day, Satan showed up with his fear-induced question tailored for Jesus: "If you are the Son of God ..." (Matt. 4:3, 6). Satan tried to get Jesus to perform miracles at his command by suggesting that he was only *really* the Son of God if he proved himself to Satan. At one point, Satan even used Scripture to try to distort its meaning like he did with Eve and with Job's friends, all with the goal of generating fear within Jesus in hopes he would lose perspective.

I often wonder if Satan and God had a Job-like meeting in heaven about Jesus. If so, I imagine it was way more intense, because Jesus' victory meant Satan would have to contend with the Holy Spirit.

Jesus was tired, yet he allowed Satan to take him to different places to tempt him. Jesus, who was both fully human and fully God, had to contend with his own amygdala firing off all the warning signs, just like we do. He had to wrestle with fears and doubts. He was hungry and exhausted. He also had the ultimate power to turn Satan into dust, Thanos-style, with one snap of his finger—but he didn't.

Jesus' trial of temptation from Satan came to a close on the cliff of a mountain so high they could see "all the kingdoms of the world and their glory" (4:8b). Satan tried to turn him to the Dark Side of the Force, but Jesus, even in his weariness, saw the other choice. Jesus knew fear *doesn't get the final say*! Although fear had brought him to a place where he understood Job's human plight and the plight of so many others who have suffered physically, emotionally, and spiritually, he gained the wisdom of his place with God and his will on earth as it is in heaven. And he never sinned.

Fear might cause you to ask, *Why me? Why them? Why now? What if?* You may complain and question God when fear overwhelms you. Satan may try to accuse you of being faithless and sinful, and distort the truth of fear as a failure. But when fear becomes your ally, fear empowers you to choose change.

The fear of the Lord perfectly positions you to see him as "a secure fortress, and for [your] children ... a refuge" (Prov. 14:26

NIV). In other words, in a world where you are vulnerable to be hurt by others, you are *safe* with God. "The fear of the LORD is the beginning of wisdom, and knowledge of the Holy One is understanding" (Prov. 9:10 NIV). Not only is God with you, but he empowers you with his wisdom and guides you in understanding through the power of the Holy Spirit.

Although the choice is yours, you never have to decide alone. "Don't be wise in your own eyes; fear the LORD and turn away from evil" (Prov. 3:7 CSB). God promises that he will be with you. Even Job, after all he had been through, said, "I know that you can do all things; no purpose of yours can be thwarted" (Job 42:2 NIV). God will strengthen you. He will help you. He will hold you.

Will fear try to rob you of saying yes to new opportunities? Absolutely! Will trusting people in relationships be risky? Always. But the treasure of trusting God and growing a heart willing to risk, show grace, and grow in wisdom and understanding far outweighs living a life stuck in fear.

Let's go cliff jumping!

CYCLE-BREAKING PRAYER

Jesus, I ask for your help in identifying the fears in my life that may be hindering my relationships with others and with you. Help me see fear in light of who you are. Give me the perspective of fear becoming an ally. Bring me to a place of deep trust in you, knowing that your love and grace are sufficient to conquer all my fears. Restore a healthy fear of you, God. Help me lean on you, trusting in your guidance and finding peace in your presence. In your name, amen.

8

BREAK THE CYCLE OF HIDDENNESS

Justin Davis

We play several variations of hiding and finding games with children.

The first and simplest is "peek-a-boo." Peek-a-boo is a deceptive game, in which we put our hands over our face and pretend that that keeps us from seeing our child. Then, we open our hands and say, "Peek-a-boo, I see you."

In teaching our kids this game, when they put their hands over their face, we say, "Where did she go? I can't see you!" Then they open their hands, and we say, "There you are! I see you."

When kids graduate from peek-a-boo, they're ready to play "hide-and-go-seek." In hide-and-go-seek, there are usually multiple hiders and one seeker. The hiders split up and find hiding places, while the seeker counts. After counting to a predetermined number, they go and find as many hiders as possible. The person found last wins and becomes the seeker in the next round.

A variation of this game is called "Sardines." Sardines starts with one hider and multiple seekers. After the seekers count, they split up and look for the person hiding. Any seeker who finds the hider joins them in the hiding place. The game ends when everyone is crammed like sardines into the hiding place.

From an early age, we make a game out of hiding and trying not to be found. But when it comes to our relationships and the repeated dysfunctional cycles we experience, hiding isn't just a game; it becomes a lifestyle.

Despite being separated in 2005, Trish and I were both committed to restoring our marriage. For that to happen, I needed to become a person of truth so I could rebuild trust. Since much of my life in that season involved hiding and distorting truth, I didn't know where to start, and I was fearful I wouldn't be able to detach myself from the comfort of hiding and pretending. In one of my first individual counseling sessions, my counselor, Dan, asked, "Can you remember a time when you were told it was okay to lie?"

I shared with you in chapter 4 that my parents got divorced in 2009 after thirty-six years of marriage. So many blessings came out of their relationship—specifically, my three siblings. But, looking back, their divorce was probably thirty years too late.

By the time a relationship ends publicly, it's been eroding privately for quite some time. What finally caused my parents' divorce was the discovery of overt and damaging choices by my dad to repeatedly cheat on my mom. It was like a thirty-six-year game of hide-and-seek that my mom didn't know she was playing—and we didn't know we were being taught.

As a teenager in the early '90s, there wasn't much to do in Crawfordsville, Indiana. Weekend fun revolved around two main activities: Friday night football and cruising the mall and McDonald's parking lots. In this pre-Amazon era, even smaller towns like Crawfordsville had shopping malls. Our mall was anchored by two stores, Sears and JCPenney. The out lot of the mall had a McDonald's, which was the hangout hub for teenagers on Friday nights. After a home football game, we would get in our cars and drive to the mall parking lot. Some would park and talk, but most would "cruise." This involved driving a circular path that started at the JCPenney side of the mall and went to the Sears side of the mall and then looped through the McDonald's parking lot before going back to begin again at JCPenney.

While my dad had a lot of faults, he loved his kids, despite his brokenness. He worked hard and sacrificed a lot to provide for our family. Even though I had a job that was required by my parents to pay for my gas and car insurance, my dad was very generous when he had extra money to give me for those Friday night cruises through the mall parking lot.

There were several occasions as I was leaving to go to a football game when my dad would say to me, "Do you have enough money?" No matter how much money I had, I would usually say, "I could always use more." He would say, "Here is $10; *don't tell your mom I gave it to you.*" My dad had a place in his wallet where he hid money.

It would be folded up several times until the bill was a small square that could be easily hidden. He pulled it out like it was top secret.

When I was sixteen years old, I didn't see the pattern he was creating in my mind. With the words, "Don't tell your mom I gave it to you," he was saying that it would cause problems if my mom found out about the money and that I needed to protect him and their relationship by keeping it secret.

As my counselor asked me this pivotal question, "Can you remember a time when you were told it was okay to lie?" I was instantly transported back to my sophomore year of high school. I could picture myself taking the secretive $10 bill, while adopting the premise that it's okay to hide things that can cause problems.

Hiddenness became a repeated pattern in my life. I hid the music I listened to with explicit lyrics. I hid the way I talked around my friends. I hid the cheating I did to get a B on my chemistry test. I hid the sexual choices I made with my girlfriend on the weekends. I hid anything that would make my parents think less of me or cause problems in our relationship.

When Trish and I got married, I didn't want to hide anything from her. But I didn't want to cause problems in our marriage either. So, in an effort to spare my marriage pain, I hid the sexual abuse I experienced as a child. I hid the pornography addiction I had the first ten years of our marriage. I hid the insecurity, fear, and inadequacy I frequently felt as a husband and father. It was a game of hide-and-go-seek that I mastered until I couldn't stay hidden any longer.

In Genesis 2, God created the heavens and the earth. Then, he looked at all that he made and said, "It is good." On the sixth day, he created Adam, but said, "It's not good for man to be alone," so he created woman.

Adam and Eve had a unique relationship with God. They were fully exposed before God, and they felt entirely comfortable. They were naked and not ashamed. They were fully known, and they felt fully loved. Imagine a relationship where there is no shame. There is no compulsion to cover up. There is no desire to hide. You are fully exposed, and you feel fully loved.

God's desire for you is that you would be fully known and know that you are fully loved.

God created this incredible home for Adam and Eve. He gave them all they could ever need, and he gave them purpose, meaning, and his presence. Then he said they could have anything they wanted in the garden, but the one thing they couldn't have was the tree in the middle of the garden. He told them to stay away from it, or they would die. It wasn't good for them.

But, as we saw in Genesis, the serpent appeared and twisted God's words to tempt Eve to question God's goodness. She began to believe that God was holding out on her and keeping her from all the fun.

> The woman was convinced. She saw that the tree was beautiful and its fruit looked delicious, and she wanted the wisdom it would give her. So she took some of the fruit and ate it. Then she gave some to her husband, who was with her, and he ate it, too. At that moment their eyes were opened, and they suddenly felt shame at their nakedness. So they sewed fig leaves together to cover themselves.

When the cool evening breezes were blowing, the man and his wife heard the LORD God walking about in the garden. So they hid from the LORD God among the trees. Then the LORD God called to the man, "Where are you?"

He replied, "I heard you walking in the garden, so I hid. I was afraid because I was naked."

"Who told you that you were naked?" the LORD God asked. "Have you eaten from the tree whose fruit I commanded you not to eat?"

The man replied, "It was the woman you gave me who gave me the fruit, and I ate it."

Then the LORD God asked the woman, "What have you done?"

"The serpent deceived me," she replied. "That's why I ate it." (Gen. 3:6–13)

Why did Adam hide? "I heard you walking in the garden, so I hid. I was afraid because I was naked" (Gen. 3:10).

David, as a boy, was set apart to be the king of Israel and the spiritual leader of God's people. From the time David slayed a giant as a boy to the time of his becoming king over all of Israel, God was with David and blessed him.

In 2 Samuel 11, it was spring "when kings normally go out to war" (v. 1). But David wasn't on the battlefield; he was in the palace. One afternoon, David was on the roof of his palace and saw a woman bathing. Captivated by her beauty, he sent one of his messengers to find out more about this woman. His messenger returned to explain that she was the wife of Uriah, a faithful soldier in the Israelite army who was away at war, fighting for David.

At this moment, David 100 percent knew who Bathsheba was. In 1 Chronicles 11, Uriah the Hittite was listed as one of David's mighty warriors. Uriah was one of thirty men who had fought with and for David in the most epic of battles. Uriah was very close—in proximity, if not regular camaraderie—to David.

But even with this new information, David overlooked what Uriah had done for him and made a really poor decision. You are probably familiar with this story: David sent for Bathsheba, leveraged his authority as the king, and slept with her. *No one will know*, he thought. He was the king and had the power to keep things quiet. But sin has a way of revealing itself, even when we think we can hide it. In time, Bathsheba realized she was pregnant.

David decided to continue lying rather than telling the truth. David called Uriah back from battle, invited him to the palace, and then sent him home to sleep with his wife so David could cover up the pregnancy. But Uriah was so loyal to the king that he refused to go home. The next day, David invited Uriah back to the palace to convince him to go home and sleep with his wife—even getting him drunk—but again, Uriah refused out of loyalty to David and his fellow soldiers. Finally, David was forced to escalate his cover-up scheme, and he had Uriah put on the front lines of the battle so he would be killed.

When David committed adultery, he not only covered up what he did from those around him, but even worse, he hid from God. Like Adam and Eve in the garden, David attempted to deal with sin by hiding it.

Why Do You Hide?

In the last chapter, Trisha talked about the danger responses of fear. That fear keeps us stuck in destructive choices. Fear and hiding go hand in hand. There is always a cause and effect when we allow fear to drive our lives. Sin causes distance in relationships. Hiding keeps distance in relationships. Sin causes pain in relationships. Hiding keeps a relationship broken. Sin causes a disconnection with God. Hiding keeps us disconnected from God. Sin affects those in our immediate circle. Hiding can impact generations.

Fear of Being Exposed

When we hide, we don't experience intimacy in the way God intended. The word *intimacy* means "to be fully known." It's the picture of God walking with Adam and Eve in the cool of the day. It's the image of them being naked but not feeling shame. That is intimacy.

When you hide from God or from someone you love, you place a lid on the amount of intimacy you're capable of experiencing. When we fear being found out, we withhold the truth from those we care about most. That fear overtakes our hearts, and we feel stress. We imagine worst-case scenarios and allow the fear of being found out to do more damage to relationships than simply being honest. Most of the time, trying to hide the truth only leads us to what we fear the most—being found out.

Fear of Rejection

As we work with couples who are working through patterns of lying, compromising truth, and broken trust, the most common reason they repeat these cycles is fear of not being loved. They believe that if their spouse knew the truth about them, they would be rejected and not loved, and their spouse would, at best, think less of them and, at worst, leave them.

Our greatest desire is to be known. Our greatest fear is that God and others won't love us. So often, we compromise being known on the altar of being loved. We can only be loved to the extent that we are known. So, every time we sacrifice honesty for acceptance, we limit our capacity to be truly loved. We know in our hearts that God or another person isn't loving the real us.

Fear of Pain

We don't want to come out of hiding, because we've calculated the emotional pain our secrets, lies, addictions, insecurities, or confessions will cause. We have concluded that the emotional pain we will endure, or cause, will be greater than any good that could come from being exposed. So, we continue to hide. We pretend things are better than they are, thinking we are sparing ourselves and those we love from emotional pain. We are convinced that if we are exposed, and if our secret is found out, the emotional distress it will cause would make us unlovable.

Finding out my dad wasn't my biological father was earthshaking to me, and it took me several months to find healing. At the time, my mom told me who my biological father was, and although I didn't know him personally, he'd had proximity to my family my entire life.

I decided not to meet or reach out to him at that point. My rationale wasn't based only on the pain I was experiencing. I knew he had other kids, and I didn't want them to experience the total upheaval of their life that I'd experienced.

A few years later, I received a call letting me know that my biological father had been diagnosed with terminal brain cancer. He had a few months to live; if I wanted to meet him, now was the time. A few weeks later, Trish and two of our three boys traveled to the assisted living facility and spent about two hours with him.

He sat with us and told us stories of his childhood, walked us through his high school yearbook, and showed us pictures of himself as a young man. He was genuine and heartfelt. At the end of our time, he apologized for all I'd been through. All of that was healing, but I had a huge issue: I didn't think he was my father.

He was barely 5' 9" and looked nothing like me. I am 6' 3". As we went through his pictures, I saw no resemblance to him as a kid, no likeness to what he looked like in high school. Our hands weren't similar, and our facial structure was completely different. I was convinced, walking out of the nursing home, that he wasn't my dad.

I called my mom immediately after we got in the car, asking, "Who else is there? There has to be someone else. He isn't the guy." My bluntness took my mom by surprise. She assured me that this was my biological father.

In the summer of 2021, I received a call that my uncle passed away. My aunt asked if I would do the graveside service for my uncle, and I agreed. Because of the proximity that my biological dad had to my family, my half brother and sister would be at the funeral. I would meet them for the first time.

As I was walking to the head of the casket at the cemetery, a lady approached me with her hand extended and introduced herself as my sister. I quickly shook her hand and opened my arms to offer a hug instead of a handshake. That embrace helped soften the awkwardness both of us felt at that moment. Later, at lunch, I got more acquainted with the brother and sister I hadn't met. I exchanged cell phone numbers with my sister and left feeling some closure.

A few weeks after the funeral, the feeling I had when I met my biological father returned. I couldn't shake it. I didn't think he was my father. I texted my new sister and asked if she would do AncestryDNA with me. She agreed, so I purchased two kits, and we both sent in our samples. About six weeks later, she texted me that her family tree had been posted and asked if I'd received my results. I told her my results were back as well.

We weren't related. There was no hint of her on my family tree and no hint of me on her family tree. I was devastated and validated all at the same time.

On July 14, 2021, I took a deep breath, opened up the AncestryDNA app, and sent a direct message to a complete stranger that DNA was telling me was my second cousin. "Hey Toni, my name is Justin Davis, and I just received results from my AncestryDNA, which listed you as my second cousin. I'm trying to discover the connection as I just found out a few years ago, at age 36, that I am adopted. Could you help me? I don't know who my biological father is, but I think you are related to him."

Then, six days later, Trish received the conclusive results from a paternity test that confirmed that her dad wasn't her biological father. If I close my eyes, I can still see the look on her face and hear the wailing cries of hurt and despair. She was devastated, and there was nothing I could do to help. It was overwhelming and disorienting.

When it comes to hiddenness, we can choose the redemptive pain of honesty or the destructive pain of hiddenness. Pastor Andy Stanley said, "We fear the consequences of confession because we've yet to experience the consequences of concealment."[1]

There is a well-known saying in Alcoholics Anonymous: "You are only as sick as your secrets." In a 2023 article, Natalie Baker said, "This basically means that a secret kept in the dark grows and becomes more harmful, but once it is exposed to light or released, its power is lost."[2]

Relationship Icebergs

At this point in the book, it's safe to tell you a secret about me. (How many more secrets can I share?) This secret is less heavy: I cry at everything. My kids make fun of me because I've been known to cry during commercials, movie previews, and Instagram Reels. When you have three biological sons who grow up with a dad who cries, it's not that big of a deal. Adopting two kids at ages seven and nine who have never had a dad, it is something to behold and make fun of.

When our oldest son, Micah, was a freshman in high school, he asked me to watch a TV show with him about a group of school counselors who went into high schools troubled by cliques and bullying. These counselors spent the day with students, and by the end, everyone was crying, hugging, and restored. He said, "Dad, this show is so powerful; you'll bawl your eyes out."

In one of the first episodes, we watched one of the counselors reference an iceberg and how what is visible above the surface is only a small representation of what is below the surface. That statement made me think about the destructive cycle of hiddenness that plagues many of our closest relationships.

Imagine with me that your life is like an iceberg. Your family relationships, friendships, work and school relationships, marriage, and relationship with God all make up this iceberg.

What's dangerous about icebergs is that what lies below the surface is usually larger than what can be seen above the waterline. The part of an iceberg that isn't visible has the potential to do the most damage. The same is true in our lives. Each relational level of our lives is like a waterline, and as we allow that waterline to lower, more of who we are is exposed to others and God.

Unlike icebergs, the waterline in our lives is totally within our control. How high or low we allow the waterline to go will determine the intimacy we can experience in our relationships and with God.

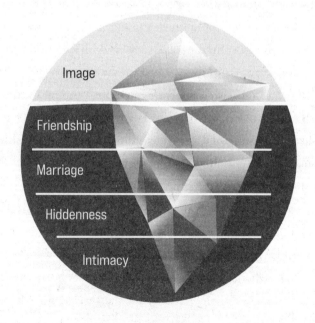

The first waterline in our lives we might call "image." The image waterline is the level we work hard to make appealing. This waterline leaves the part of the iceberg above the surface that everyone sees. It represents the most visible and public parts of your life. This is your job. This is the car you drive. This is the house you live in. This is the smile you put on your face on the way to church. This is what your golfing buddies think about you. This is the school you want your kids to go to. This is the neighborhood you aspire to live in. This is the public persona you display for those you want to impress. This is what your neighbors think about you. This is the area of your life that you try hard to make respectable and noticeable. This is what you allow many of your relationships to know about you. This is the surface level of our lives.

There is a second waterline in most of our lives. This is the relationship waterline. This waterline represents what your friends know about you. More of your heart is exposed when you allow others to see your life at this waterline. This waterline is reserved for a select group of people in your life. It allows a smaller group of people to know more about you. They know your successes as well as your failures. They know your dreams and your hopes. At this waterline, you share your story and go beyond the exterior you've cultivated. The smaller group at this waterline is allowed to see your dysfunctions and weaknesses.

If you are married, your relationship with your spouse likely starts to deepen. The waterline probably started high when you were dating. Your spouse could do no wrong. She was perfect; you never fought, he didn't know your past, and she didn't know your flaws.

But then there was a shift, and you realized that you could trust this person, be more vulnerable with him or her, and share more of yourself. As your relationship grew, you consciously decided to allow the person you were dating to become the person you would marry. You lowered the waterline; you exposed more of your heart.

The next waterline is marriage. This is the waterline reserved for your spouse. It is the most intimidating waterline and leaves your heart exposed and vulnerable. You envisioned your spouse knowing everything about you and you knowing everything about your spouse. This is the part of your heart that you allow only your spouse to see.

When people stand at the altar and say, "I do," they don't anticipate there being another waterline. At that moment, they believe that the marriage relationship would have the safety and security to be fully known, fully exposed, and have no part of their life below the waterline.

But the longer we are married, the easier it is to allow the waterline of our hearts to creep back up and leave more and more of our hearts below the surface, not visible even to our spouses.

There is another waterline in most of our lives. This waterline isn't dependent on marital status. It is called "hiddenness," and this is the part of our hearts that we don't allow anyone to see. This is the part of our hearts where we withhold the truth. This is that part of our hearts where we say:

If they ever knew that about me, they wouldn't love me.

If he knew I struggled with that, our relationship would be over.

If she knew I had a one-night stand in college, she wouldn't forgive me.

If they knew I was abused as a child, they would think less of me.

We want to experience the fullness of intimacy with God and others, but we don't want to share all of our heart. Being fully known will often cost us more than we are willing to give. So, we settle with being partially known, and as a result, we feel partially loved.

In his book *Attacking Anxiety*, Pastor Shawn Johnson said this:

> At their core, every human being wants to be fully known, fully loved, and fully accepted. We want to be understood. We want to be validated. We just want to know that we are okay. Unfortunately, none of those things are possible unless we are willing to let people into our lives. If we want to be fully loved, we have to be willing to be fully known.[3]

For most of us, we reach a point where we think we can hide this part of our hearts from others, and from God too. If we can go to church enough, be spiritual enough, read our Bibles enough, and be good enough, then maybe God won't notice the parts of our hearts we have yet to expose to him.

The first requirement to break the cycle of hiddenness is to understand why we hide. We hide because we are fearful of not being loved and accepted. If we don't know why we hide, we will continue the cycle of dishonesty in our relationships. Finally, we must know where we hide.

Where Do You Hide?

Adam and Eve hid behind fig leaves.

David hid in the palace while his mighty men were on the battlefield.

My dad hid $10 from my mom in his wallet.

Our moms hid our identity in the past.

We all have a hiding place. You have a hiding place. You have a place to go to escape your sin. You have a place you go running from your secrets. We all have a hiding place.

Achievement

We don't typically think of achieving as a negative thing. Achievement in and of itself isn't negative until it becomes ultimate. For some of us, we hide behind our titles. We hide behind our tax bracket. We hide behind our subdivision or the zip code we live in. We have to sell the most. We have to be the best room mom. We have to plan the perfect one-year-old birthday party. We hide behind all we can achieve.

Addiction

Addictive behavior is usually a response to a void in our life. Maybe you hide behind alcohol. You started drinking to take the edge off, but now it's a pattern of behavior you can't get through an evening without. Maybe it's a drug addiction or a pornography addiction. Perhaps it's an addiction to online gambling. What started as an innocent place to find relief has become a constrictive place to hide.

Escape

Escapism is when someone routinely uses an activity or behavior to escape life's realities. In my experience, it's taking things that can be healthy and making them a means of coping with pain. Netflix isn't bad, but it can be a means of escape. Playing Xbox Live isn't unhealthy until you use it to disassociate from reality. Dating relationships can be healthy until you go from relationship to relationship or one-night stand to one-night stand as a means of escape. Retail therapy has its place until it becomes necessary to deal with the stress or hurt in your life.

In his book, *The Thing Beneath the Thing*, Steve Carter said:

> Whenever Christ invites us to lean in and instead we do all we can to leap out, we forfeit intimacy with him. We are settling for the fast and fake instead of waiting in trust for the real thing. It is much, much harder to slow down, admit a mistake, confess a sin, or let ourselves be seen as less than perfect. Sadly, many of us have received the message that to be loved we must keep parts of ourselves hidden, so we work to conceal those parts. As much as we desire the transforming power of Jesus to do a new work in us, this takes time, intentionality, and honesty.[4]

One of the reasons we experience repeated cycles in our relationships is because we are unwilling to lower the waterline in our life and be honest with ourselves and others about why we hide or where we hide. We are embarrassed, fearful, or ashamed, and that keeps us disconnected and isolated. There is another way to live. We can live fully known and fully loved.

We are okay with letting people in on 90 percent of our struggles, but it's the last 10 percent—the real dark places, deep pain, and desperate thoughts—that we are too embarrassed to ever say out loud. That's the stuff we consider humiliating. That's the stuff we want to take to our graves.[5]

Brennan Manning said this in *Abba's Child*:

> Only in a relationship of the deepest intimacy can we allow another person to know us as we truly are. It is difficult enough for us to live with the awareness of our stinginess and shallowness, our anxieties and infidelities, but to disclose our dark secrets to another is intolerably risky. The impostor does not want to come out of hiding. He will grab for the cosmetic kit and put on his pretty face to make himself "presentable."[6]

Let's go back to the story of David. He had already committed adultery and murder. The king of Israel—in no uncertain terms—had sinned. Not only had he sinned, but he had also hidden his sin from God. For almost an entire year, this sin went unconfessed. Finally, God had enough, and he went to confront David.

In 2 Samuel 12, we read how God sent the prophet Nathan to confront David's sin, to lower the waterline of his heart, and expose the iceberg he'd been hiding:

> So the LORD sent Nathan the prophet to tell David this story: "There were two men in a certain town. One was rich, and one was poor. The rich man owned a great many sheep and cattle. The poor man owned nothing but one little lamb he had bought. He raised that little lamb, and it grew up with his children. It ate from the man's own plate and drank from his cup. He cuddled it in his arms like a baby daughter. One day a guest arrived at the home of the rich man. But instead of killing an animal from his own flock or herd, he took the poor man's lamb and killed it and prepared it for his guest."
>
> David was furious. "As surely as the LORD lives," he vowed, "any man who would do such a thing deserves to die! He must repay four lambs to the poor man for the one he stole and for having no pity."
>
> Then Nathan said to David, "You are that man!" (vv.1–7)

This is what I love about the story of David: with those four words—"You are that man!"—his entire life was exposed. The waterline was lowered. Most of the time, like David, we, too, wait until we are told before we realize the tremendous freedom in coming out of hiding. David was exposed, and in the process of being exposed, he discovered the power of confession.

Look what David said in Psalm 32:1–7 (NIV):

> Blessed is the one
>   whose transgressions are forgiven,
>   whose sins are covered.
> Blessed is the one
>   whose sin the LORD does not count against them
>   and in whose spirit is no deceit.
>
> When I kept silent,
>   my bones wasted away
>   through my groaning all day long.
> For day and night
>   your hand was heavy on me;
> my strength was sapped
>   as in the heat of summer.
>
> Then I acknowledged my sin to you
>   and did not cover up my iniquity.
> I said, "I will confess
>   my transgressions to the LORD."
> And you forgave
>   the guilt of my sin.

Therefore let all the faithful pray to you
    while you may be found;
surely the rising of the mighty waters
    will not reach them.
You are my hiding place;
    you will protect me from trouble
    and surround me with songs of deliverance.

Maybe you are in a similar place to the one David was in. You are wasting away because you are silent about your sin. You have secrets, mistakes, and things you have convinced yourself that you can never confess. You are repeating the same sin because you have yet to confess it. You are tired.

Did you catch what David said near the end of that last passage? "You are my hiding place."

Life is lived differently when we stop trying to hide our sins and allow God himself to be our hiding place. When God is your hiding place, you don't have to hide. When God is your hiding place, you don't have to try to be loved; you know you are loved. When God is your hiding place, you can break the cycle that keeps you from being fully known.

CYCLE-BREAKING PRAYER

Jesus, I confess that I often hide from you and others. Too often, I let fear dictate my choices, which has damaged my relationships. Please help me identify why I hide and where I hide. Give me the courage to embrace your grace, the only source of true transformation and healing. Guide me to be open and authentic, trusting in your strength and love to mend my heart and restore intimacy with others. In your name, amen.

9

BREAK THE CYCLE OF SHAME

Justin Davis

Before Trisha and I wrote our first book, *Beyond Ordinary: When a Good Marriage Just Isn't Good Enough,* we shared our story on our website, refineus.org. We continue to do our best to be open and honest about our mistakes, the choices we regret, and the restoration and redemption God brought to our relationship. But we go first so others feel permission to go second.

As we started sharing our story online, we began to get requests to speak and share our testimony at churches all over the country. So, in the early days of RefineUs, we would go to a church, share our testimony on a Sunday morning, and then go home.

One Sunday, we were in Tampa, Florida, and as we shared our story, you could hear cries and sobs coming from the congregation. It was heavy. We finished the second service, stood at the door talking to people for a few minutes as they left, then got in the car to go home. About thirty minutes into our trip home, Trisha said, "I don't want to do this anymore." I said, "Okay. If you don't want to share our story, we don't have to share our story."

She said, "No, that's not what I mean. We go into these churches, and all these unsuspecting people come that day not knowing what we are about to share. We talk about sexual brokenness, hiddenness, and unforgiveness, and then in the last five minutes of the message, we say, 'But God healed us, and we're doing great today. So let's close in prayer.' I don't want to do that anymore. I want to equip people to experience God's best for their marriage, not just tell them how ours imploded."

A few hours later, I got a text message from a friend from college. He said, "I heard you guys spoke at Danny's church in Tampa today. We'd love for you guys to do a marriage conference for us in October. Talk it over with Trish, and let me know."

I texted him back, "We're in. We'd love to do that." I told Trish, "Greg wants us to do a marriage conference for his church in October."

She said, "We've never done that before."

I said, "I told him we'd do it. It's February, which means we have eight months to design the content for the conference. You said you want to equip people to have the marriage God has in mind; this is our chance. God answered your prayer."

I had hoped "crediting" God would diminish Trish's anger over me agreeing to do the marriage conference without asking her, but it was a few days before her anger went away. We started working each week to develop content for the marriage conference, and the six sessions we developed became the foundation of the book we wrote two years later.

After that first conference in October 2010, God opened doors for us to travel across the country and share our marriage conference. In 2014, we received a speaking request for a church in New Hampshire. The pastor and I worked out the details: we would do two sessions on Friday night, three on Saturday morning, and speak at both of their Sunday morning church services.

About a week before the conference in New Hampshire, I posted on Facebook how excited we were to be going to New Hampshire to do our RefineUs Marriage Conference. A few minutes later, a friend texted to ask if I could talk for a few minutes. He and his wife were longtime friends of ours, and he had been at a church leadership conference where Trish and I shared our testimony.

He said, "I saw you are going to New Hampshire. I lived there for thirteen years. It is an amazing place with amazing people, but you may be a little much for some people there."

I said, "What do you mean, 'a little much'?"

He said, "The people of New England aren't as open and vulnerable as you and Trish. You have primarily spoken at churches in the Midwest and the South. The Northeast is different than what you are used to. So I want to prepare you: even if people look mad at you while you speak, they could love what you are saying."

When we arrived at the church, the pastor gave us a tour of the church, set us up with audio and video, did a mic check, and then we went back to his office. He said, "I want to prepare you guys. Your story is open and vulnerable. It resonates with me deeply, and it's part of the reason I brought you in this weekend. But culturally, vulnerability isn't something people in the Northeast are known for."

Later, Trish and I talked through our outline for the conference's first session, and she asked me if I would adjust any content in light of what the pastor told us. I said, "I don't plan on it. I don't want to offend anyone, but I also want to be faithful to the message we are called to share." We decided to move forward as planned.

The first session of our conference was about God's vision for marriage, and in the middle of that session, I shared my choice in 2005 to have an affair with Trish's best friend. As I confessed this part of our story, a few couples got up and started walking toward the back of the room. I didn't think much of it at the time, but then a few minutes later, a few more couples got up and left. In the first thirty minutes of our first session, at least ten couples left the conference.

We closed that session in prayer and went back into the pastor's office. I was feeling very self-conscious. And the second session is significantly more intense than the first. I talk about being sexually abused as a kid and struggling with pornography for the first ten years of marriage.

When I get nervous, I sweat like crazy. I don't have hair, so there's nothing to stop sweat from streaming down my face. I was soaked with sweat trying to figure out what to do. Finally, I told Trisha, "If we don't share this truth, then we are compromising

God's call on our hearts. I'll be sensitive in sharing this session, but we should move forward."

We got back onstage and shared the content from our hearts, and by God's grace, no one else got up and left. The first night of the conference was in the books, but we had three more sessions on Saturday. We went to the hotel, wondering if anyone would come back. To our surprise, everyone who attended the first two sessions returned on Saturday.

We finished just before lunch, and as we walked off the stage, I felt exhausted and wondered if anything we said had resonated or made a difference in anyone's heart or marriage. I walked down the stairs and was met by a man in tears. He asked if he could talk to me. I guided him to an area in the auditorium where we could have more privacy.

He said, "I can't thank you enough for this weekend. God brought you here for me. God brought you here to set me free. I'm eighty-four years old, and I've been married for sixty-four years. I was sexually abused when I was ten, and I've lived in shame and guilt for the last seventy-four years. God brought you here to set me free from that shame."

I was speechless. I said, "Can I give you a hug?" He agreed, and we embraced. He hugged me like a ten-year-old boy hugs his dad.

He continued, "I've never told anyone about this until last night. After your second session, during the discussion time, I told my wife about the abuse. It felt like a weight was lifted from me."

Tears started streaming down my face; it was all I could do not to break out into weeping. I had seen this gentleman throughout the conference. His arms were often crossed. His demeanor appeared bothered or at least uninterested. But what I had interpreted as disapproval of me was his seventy-four-year battle with disapproving of himself. I had grossly misunderstood the moment.

We embraced again, and I shared some steps I'd taken to overcome the shame of my abuse and the guilt of my porn addiction. I prayed for him, and then, in a divine moment, he asked if he could pray for me. I don't remember all of it, but I remember him praying, "Heavenly Father, remind Justin that you are using his words to uncover and deconstruct shame."

I'll never forget that moment. As we start this chapter together, my hope is that you can begin to uncover and deconstruct the shame in your life.

In her 2012 TED Talk, researcher and *New York Times* bestselling author Brené Brown said, "Shame is an unspoken epidemic, the secret behind many forms of broken behavior."[1]

We can't break cycles in our lives or relationships until we stop blaming others and start taking responsibility for our choices. We can't address shame until we grieve what we've lost and deal with our unforgiveness. Until we are committed to coming out of hiding, shame will always have a place in our lives.

What Shame Isn't

Before we define *shame*, it is essential to acknowledge and define what *shame* is not.

Embarrassment

When we feel embarrassed, we feel socially foolish. This is a temporary moment in time that is most often circumstantial. In high school, I worked as a cashier at Target. I am not trying to brag, but I was an excellent cashier. If you've never been a professional cashier like me, you may not know that when you scan a customer's first item, a timer starts and continues until you hit the total button. As a cashier, you are measured and evaluated by how long it takes to move customers through your line. Part of cashier training is developing the art of carrying on conversations while at the same time maintaining efficiency in scanning and bagging the items the customer is purchasing.

One evening, a lady approached my line, and I began to scan her items. The conversation started strong. "Hey there, welcome to Target." She replied with a smile and said, "Hi."

"How are you tonight?"

"I am doing well; how are you?"

She put a few clothing items on the conveyor belt, and the belt started to move in my direction. She had at least one CD in an oversized, white plastic case, and a few cosmetic items.

She did *not* purchase anything maternity related—no maternity clothes, newborn clothes, diapers, wipes, formula, or books on having a baby. Her purchases showed no indication whatsoever that she was "with child."

But for reasons I can't explain or justify, my seventeen-year-old mouth said, "When is your baby due?"

As soon as I said it, I knew I couldn't take it back. The air seemed to be sucked out of the store. It felt like everyone stopped what they were doing and stared at me. Her smile was erased. She gazed at me with a look that pierced my soul and said, "I'm not pregnant."

I have many regrets from that incident. My biggest regret is the timing of the question. I still had several items to scan, and the conveyor belt seemed to move in slow motion. It felt like an eternity of awkward silence. I avoided making eye contact. I couldn't hit that subtotal button fast enough. After she paid, I flipped my light on and asked to go on a break. When I told my boss what I had said to the customer, she gave me the rest of the night off.

We've all felt embarrassment. In his book *Shame and Grace*, author Lewis Smedes said, "The difference [between shame and embarrassment] is … we feel embarrassed because we *look* bad, and we feel shame because we think we *are* bad."[2]

Guilt

Guilt is often confused with shame. *Guilt* is a legal term that defines reality. Its literal definition is "the fact of having committed a breach of conduct, especially violating law and involving a penalty."[3] Guilt has an attachment to a moral code of conduct. It's the admission or determination that we have done something wrong.

Pastor Louie Giglio, in a message entitled "The Chain of Shame," defined *guilt* as "the position of being accountable for our sins and our shortcomings."[4] The Greek word for *guilt* is ἔνοχος, which means "liable to or bound by." When we experience guilt, it is the emotion that is bound to the act of what we have done wrong. I do something wrong and feel bad for what I've done wrong. Guilt is based on behavior. Guilt is based on choices. Guilt can be overcome with an apology or an ask for forgiveness.

What Is Shame?

Webster's Dictionary defines *shame* as "a painful emotion caused by consciousness of guilt, shortcoming, or impropriety."[5] That is the literal definition of *shame*.

But there is also a spiritual definition. Spiritually speaking, shame goes beyond what we've done to the very core of who we are.

Shame goes beyond the transaction of emotion for what I've done wrong and seeps into the soul of who I am. Shame doesn't cause me to feel like what I've done is terrible; it convinces me that I am horrible because I've done something wrong. Shame allows me to know the freedom of forgiveness but not feel free even though I know I'm forgiven. Shame goes to the core of who I am and how I see God.

In her book *Daring Greatly*, Brené Brown distinguishes between shame and guilt in this way: "The difference between shame and guilt is best understood as the difference between 'I am bad' and 'I did something bad.'

> Guilt = I did something bad
> Shame = I am bad."[6]

Brown summarizes her years of research of shame in this definition: "Shame is the intensely painful feeling or experience of believing that we are flawed and therefore unworthy of love and belonging."[7]

Guilt is a momentary spiritual transaction. Shame is a long-standing spiritual condition. There is an epidemic of shame in the hearts and souls of followers of Jesus today. We feel shame in our friendships, shame in our marriages, shame as parents, shame as children, shame as employees, shame as employers. We accumulate guilt over time, and when our guilt is unacknowledged and unconfessed, it becomes a part of us, as shame.

Lewis Smedes gives us examples of the feeling of shame and how to identify the shame you may be unknowingly living with:

> I sometimes feel as if I am a fake.
> I feel that if people who admire me really knew me they might have contempt for me.
> I feel inadequate; I seldom feel as if I am up to what is expected of me.
> When I look inside of myself, I seldom feel any joy at what I am.
> I feel inferior to the really good people that I know.
> I feel as if God must be disgusted with me.
> I feel flawed inside, blemished somehow, dirty sometimes.
> I feel as if I just cannot measure up to what I ought to be.
> I feel as if I will never be acceptable.[8]

Why is this important? Because unacknowledged shame causes repeated, cyclical, and destructive behavior. Brené Brown said:

In my research I found that shame corrodes the very part of us that believes we can change and do better.... Shame is highly correlated with addiction, violence, aggression, depression, eating disorders, and bullying. Researchers don't find shame correlated with positive outcomes at all—there is no data to support that shame is a helpful compass for good behavior. In fact, shame is much more likely to be the cause of destructive and hurtful behaviors than it is to be the solution.[9]

How Does Shame Find Us?

Shame can be put into two categories: shame for what we've done or shame for what has been done to us. The first is about the choices we've made; the mistakes we've repeated; the sins we commit. We experience shame as the result of our misguided or destructive decisions.

The second, shame for what has been done to us, can be intentional or unintentional wounds that have been placed on us by the choices of others in our lives. You feel shame over criticism from a boss or a coach; the harsh words from a parent; the betrayal of a friendship; the abuse you didn't choose; abandonment by a spouse. In order to heal our hearts and break the cycle of shame in our relationships, we have to identify how shame finds us.

Trauma

Shame is something we all experience. There is a misconception that shame is reserved for people who have experienced trauma. While this isn't true, trauma *is* a pathway to shame.

I was sexually abused in three different seasons of my life by three different, unrelated people. The first time was when I was five years old by a neighbor across the street. The second time was by a family member when I was ten or eleven. The final time was when I was in high school by a family friend. Each of these incidents brought an element of hiddenness, humiliation, and trauma.

Shame finds us in our trauma and spews lies like, "This was your fault. You brought this on yourself. You are the type of person that abusers are attracted to. You are undeserving of love."

I don't know what trauma you are carrying that has turned into shame. Maybe you were physically or emotionally abused when you were a kid, and you convinced yourself that the abuse was your fault. You deserved it. Maybe you were sexually abused as a child, and you told someone, but they didn't believe you, or they believed you but didn't do anything about it. Maybe you were sexually assaulted in college, and you carry shame because you shouldn't have been at that party. You shouldn't have gone on that date. You should not have put yourself in that situation. That assault was your fault. Maybe your spouse cheated on you, your parent abandoned you, or your friend betrayed you. Again, shame says, "You deserved what happened to you."

Smedes said, "We deceive ourselves with the falsehood that we are unworthy human beings. We support our deception with the plausible reasons why we should feel unworthy."[10]

Family

Finding out that the dad I grew up with wasn't my biological father was shocking and disorienting. But after I had time to process this reality, a lot of my abandonment issues began to make sense. I had always felt like an outsider looking in when it came to my dad accepting me.

My dad was mechanical and loved working with his hands, because he was good at it. I am the least mechanical person alive. I wanted to help him change the oil in our car or work on the brakes, but my attempts always ended in frustration, and he would usually say, "Just go in the house with your mom." My dad loved to hunt, fish, and ride motorcycles. He connected and bonded with my brothers around those activities, and I had zero interest in hunting, fishing, or motorcycles.

I know my dad was proud of me for my sports accomplishments and of the husband and father I eventually became, but I grew up feeling ashamed that I wasn't the son he truly wanted. If I could be more of a craftsman, learn to ride a Harley-Davidson, and tolerate hunting and fishing, he might be prouder of me.

As my dad and brothers would go fishing without me (even though I didn't want to go), I would tell myself, "When I have kids, I'll never make them feel this way." As we've discussed earlier in the book, what isn't healed is often repeated.

When our son Elijah was a freshman at Indiana Wesleyan University, he wasn't taking his schoolwork as seriously as I wanted him to. With little effort, he had earned a prestigious academic scholarship, but he had to maintain a 3.0 GPA to keep the scholarship. On a Sunday night late in the semester, I was driving home from a speaking engagement and had some free time to call Elijah to give him a "pep talk" about getting his grades up before the semester ended. As we got deeper into the conversation, I compared Elijah and his work ethic with his older brother, Micah. Micah, too, was a student at Indiana Wesleyan, on basketball and academic scholarships, and had a 3.8 GPA.

I don't remember what I said, but Elijah got very emotional. He told me I made him feel less than the other two boys because he didn't play basketball. He recounted several occasions throughout his childhood when I took the boys to games, shot hoops in the driveway, and even talked more to them around the dinner table about games, players, and teams. He spent his whole life hoping I'd love him as much as I loved them. He felt like his grade point average was just another vehicle for me to communicate my disappointment with him. He knew I was ashamed of him.

Immediately, I realized what I had done. Basketball was fishing. Basketball was hunting. The shame I felt in my family all those years, I had transferred to my son. While it was a painful realization, it is one I am thankful for today. Elijah and I would never be able to break that cycle of shame without identifying it and owning it.

Our relationship with our parents informs how we process wounds and guilt that eventually become shame. Maybe, like me, you never felt accepted for who you are by your parents. Perhaps you still feel that way. Maybe your parents were a source of shame through things they said:

"You should be ashamed of yourself."

"Why can't you be more like your brother/sister?"

"You are such an idiot."

"You are disgusting."

"When are you going to make something of yourself?"

"Keep acting like that; you'll never get anyone to love you."

To break the cycle of shame, we must disconnect what was said about us from who we are. I've learned that those who project shame onto others haven't overcome it themselves. That is why this is so important. To not continue the cycle of shame in your life, you have to identify the source of your shame and disconnect it from who you are.

Religion

I don't have experience in expressions of religion other than the evangelical Church. I wish the American Church weren't such a huge source of shame, but for many, that is the case.

Religion is based on performance. The church I grew up in claimed to be a place of amazing grace but was structured around religious performance. In Sunday school, we had a chart on the wall that tracked spiritual activities like:

- attendance
- bringing your Bible
- memorizing the books of the Bible
- bringing a friend to church
- reciting that week's memory verse

For each accomplishment, we received a star. There was a sense of pride in walking to the front of the class and putting the star (or stars) next to your name. We could earn a pizza party if enough people in the class accumulated enough stars.

In fifth grade, I'll never forget being called out by my Sunday school teacher in front of the whole class for not having enough stars. I was holding the class back. I needed to live up to my potential. There was no consideration that my parents fought most Sundays all the way to church. There wasn't a desire to understand the climate of our family and the turmoil I navigated around my dad's temper. "You need more stars." "You need to be a better disciple of Jesus." "The class can't have a pizza party until you get it together."

While not always intentional, the people of Jesus have made people feel the shame that Jesus himself died to overcome. Romans 8:1–2 says, "Therefore, there is now no condemnation for those who are in Christ Jesus, because through Christ Jesus the law of the Spirit who gives life has set you free from the law of sin and death" (NIV).

The word *condemnation* in Greek means "judgment" or "to find guilty." In a 2019 survey, Lifeway Research asked 2,002 people between the ages of twenty-three and thirty why they left the evangelical Church. Thirty-two percent of them said, "Church members seem judgmental."[11]

In Christ, there is no judgment; but in Christ followers, there is condemnation. Condemnation is oxygen to shame.

Failure

Shame comes to us in what has been done to us or projected on us. But often, shame makes a home in our heart through failure. Our failures aren't a reflection of our intentions; they are the result of our choices. Each of the gospel writers recorded a conversation with Jesus and Peter on the night Jesus was arrested. Peter had good intentions, followed by the doubling down of a sincere promise, but the result was failure:

> On the way [to the garden of Gethsemane], Jesus told them, "All of you will desert me. For the Scriptures say, 'God will strike the Shepherd, and the sheep will be scattered.' But after I am raised from the dead, I will go ahead of you to Galilee and meet you there." Peter said to him, "Even if everyone else deserts you, I never will." Jesus replied, "I tell you the truth, Peter—this very night, before the rooster crows twice, you will deny three times that you even know me." "No!" Peter declared emphatically. "Even if I have to die with you, I will never deny you!" And all the others vowed the same. (Mark 14:27–31)

Jesus was just a few hours from being crucified. One of the Twelve had already betrayed him, and he knew another would deny him. Peter was one of Jesus' closest friends. He promised loyalty, devotion, and faithfulness. He said he would die before denying Jesus. As soon as Jesus was arrested, though, the promises immediately started to fade: "Then all his disciples deserted him and ran away" (Mark 14:50).

Peter found himself standing outside, warming his hands over a campfire, while Jesus began his first trial of the night.

> Meanwhile, Peter was in the courtyard below. One of the servant girls who worked for the high priest came by and noticed Peter warming himself at the fire. She looked at him closely and said, "You were one of those with Jesus of Nazareth."
>
> But Peter denied it. "I don't know what you're talking about," he said, and he went out into the entryway. Just then, a rooster crowed. (Mark 14:66–68)

Peter had every intention of sticking with Jesus, but he deserted him. He had great intentions of being loyal until death, then abandoned him. But Peter wasn't done denying Jesus by the fire.

> When the servant girl saw him standing there, she began telling the others, "This man is definitely one of them!" But Peter denied it again.
>
> A little later some of the other bystanders confronted Peter and said, "You must be one of them, because you are a Galilean."
>
> Peter swore, "A curse on me if I'm lying—I don't know this man you're talking about!" And immediately the rooster crowed the second time. (Mark 14:69–72)

Suddenly, Jesus' words flashed through Peter's mind: "Before the rooster crows, you will deny

three times that you even know me." And he went
away, weeping bitterly. (Matt. 26:75)

Failing after promising not to fail carries a heavy weight of
shame.

You promised you would be faithful, and then you cheated.

You promised you would be loyal, and then you gossiped.

You promised you would be truthful, and then you lied.

You promised you would be pure, and then you looked at porn
again.

You promised you would control your temper, and then you lost
it again on those you love most.

Shame draws its greatest power through the current of our
failures. Guilt is accountability for our sin and shortcomings.
Shame is the process of reshaping our identity around our sin and
shortcomings.[12]

The consequences of shame are the very things that make it
cyclical—disconnection and isolation. Shame robs us from the joy
and safety of belonging. What was Peter's response to his failure? He
ran away weeping.

Remembering that shame is the fear of disconnection—the
fear that we're unlovable and don't belong—reveals why so many
people in midlife overfocus on their children's lives, work sixty hours
a week, or turn to affairs, addiction, and disengagement. We start
to unravel. The expectations and messages that fuel shame keep us
from fully realizing who we are as people.[13]

The Voice of Shame

If you have failed in your marriage, in a friendship, as a parent, or in your role at work, the voice of shame whispers often into your soul. *You are not worthy. You are not loved. You are not valued. You'll never amount to anything. You'll always struggle with this. You'll always be single. You'll never be a good parent. You'll always be in debt. You'll never be free from this addiction. You'll always be a cheater. You can't be forgiven. You will never be enough. You will never be trustworthy.*

In her book *I Shouldn't Feel This Way*, Dr. Alison Cook said:

> And so we become masters of beating ourselves up.... We replay the loop of guilt messages in our minds until we're exhausted. And in the face of exhaustion, the noise in our minds intensifies. We continue to move forward amidst the swirling truth-splinters, doing exactly what we've been doing up to this point. We avoid, procrastinate, self-criticize, or self-gaslight, and then, of course, we numb.
>
> Reach for the phone.
>
> Reach for the chips.
>
> Reach for someone else's problems to fix....
>
> When we don't stop and face the chaos in our minds, we stay stuck.[14]

Breaking the Cycle of Shame

If we are going to break the cycle of shame that damages our hearts and diminishes our relational connectedness, we have to move beyond being sorry.

My sister, Meredith, and I have a great relationship today, but growing up, we were like oil and water. We argued a lot, and both felt justified in our treatment of each other. If a disagreement went too far or if one of us got physical with the other, my mom would step in with a reconciliation plan. She would get two chairs and sit them facing each other. I would sit in one chair, my sister in the other. The mandate was simple: sit in these chairs, toe to toe, knee to knee, eye to eye, until one of you apologizes.

The first couple of times, I was too stubborn to give in. We sat in those chairs for a few hours, neither wanting the other person to win. Finally, I would apologize. But after a few rounds, I realized this could be a speedy process. I didn't have to mean I was sorry; I just had to say it. So, I didn't view it as a loss but a strategic move to continue my day, even if I wasn't sorry.

Many of us repeat behavior in our relationships because we are only sorry we got caught, we are sorry our choice hurt someone else, or we are sorry that what we did interrupted our evening with an argument—but we aren't remorseful. Sorrow without remorse adds up to regret.

Researchers have found that the most common human emotion is love. That isn't all that surprising.

But what might be surprising is that regret is the second most common human emotion.

"If only I would have gone to counseling instead of filing for divorce."

"If only I'd spent more time with my kids when they were growing up."

"If only I'd offered forgiveness to my dad before he passed away."

"If only" is the mantra of regret.

All pain stings, but regret has a unique sting. It's not just, "I wish things had turned out differently"; it's "I know things could have turned out differently if I would have acted other than the way that I did."

What do you do with your regret? Scripture has one word to overcome your regret and release you from shame: *repentance*. Repentance is the pathway to overcoming regret and breaking the cycle of shame.

Repentance is a big word used in church, but it means a sincere sorrow for wrongdoing and turning in the opposite direction. Paul talked about this in his letter to the Corinthians.

To give you some background, the church in Corinth was a mess. Paul had sent them a letter and just went after them. We don't know what the letter said, but he must have taken off the gloves, because he admitted it was harsh and direct, and it hurt the church in Corinth. So that is the context for what he wrote in 2 Corinthians 7:

> Even if I caused you sorrow by my letter, I do not regret it. Though I did regret it—I see that my letter hurt you, but only for a little while—yet now I am happy, not because you were made sorry, but because your sorrow led you to repentance. For you became

sorrowful as God intended and so were not harmed in any way by us. Godly sorrow brings repentance that leads to salvation and leaves no regret, but worldly sorrow brings death (vv. 8–10 NIV).

Being "made sorry" is, at best, a guilt trip, and at worst, manipulation. Godly sorrow is conviction. *Conviction* is a legal word that means "the act or process of finding a person guilty." Spiritually speaking, when followers of Jesus feel conviction, it is the work of the Holy Spirit to bring godly sorrow to our hearts to lead us to repentance. Godly sorrow brings life (salvation) and leaves no regret. Worldly sorrow is shame, brings death, and causes us to repeat destructive cycles in our relationships.

Let's go back to the night before the crucifixion. Peter had denied knowing Jesus after promising to die for him. Luke recorded an intimate detail in Luke 22:61: "At that moment the Lord turned and looked at Peter." Jesus was in Caiaphas's house, and at the precise moment of Peter's denial, the rooster crowed. Jesus, likely looking out the window, locked eyes with the apostle. This failure was personal.

On the morning of the resurrection, Peter heard that Jesus was alive and had risen from the dead. He took off in a dead sprint to see if it was true. He was hopeful to see Jesus, because the last time he had seen him was in the midst of his denial. Jesus appeared to the disciples two times, but no personal conversation between Jesus and Peter is recorded.

Jesus asked the disciples to return to Galilee and said he would meet them there in a few days. The disciples went back to Galilee and were in their boats fishing on the Sea of Galilee when Jesus appeared on the shore. He told them to throw their nets over to the other side of the boat, and they immediately caught 153 fish. John then recognized that it was Jesus on the shore. Peter jumped out of the boat and ran to Jesus. Then Jesus issued an invitation to Peter that he gives you today:

"Now come and have some breakfast!" (John 21:12).

No accusations.

No interrogation.

No allegation or incrimination. Just an invitation to a meal.

Two Fires

The fire of shame is fed by silence, judgment, and secrecy; left to burn, it can damage all aspects of our lives. And yet, it doesn't have to be this way; empathy has the potential to put out the flames, turn down the heat, and stop throwing fuel on the fire.[15]

In her work on shame, Brené Brown talked about *shame triggers* and how they can propel us into dark places of isolation, hiddenness, and disconnection from community.[16] Peter denied Jesus three times around a campfire. After his resurrection, Jesus invited Peter back into belonging and relationship around a campfire. Jesus wanted the campfire to trigger for Peter the memory of friendship, not failure.

> After breakfast Jesus asked Simon Peter, "Simon son of John, do you love me more than these?"

"Yes, Lord," Peter replied, "you know I love you."

"Then feed my lambs," Jesus told him.

Jesus repeated the question: "Simon son of John, do you love me?"

"Yes, Lord," Peter said, "you know I love you."

"Then take care of my sheep," Jesus said.

A third time he asked him, "Simon son of John, do you love me?"

Peter was hurt that Jesus asked the question a third time. He said, "Lord, you know everything. You know that I love you."

Jesus said, "Then feed my sheep." (John 21:15–17)

Three denials of friendship. Three questions of redemption.

Do you love me? Jesus reclaimed Peter's memories.

Do you love me? Jesus reconnected Peter to community.

Do you love me? Jesus redefined Peter's calling.

How is shame impacting your relationships? Are you willing to move beyond being sorry and be remorseful? Are you ready to invite the conviction of the Holy Spirit to lead you to repentance? Are you ready to burn your regret in the campfire of redemption? Jesus is inviting you to come have some breakfast.

CYCLE-BREAKING PRAYER

Jesus, I bring you the burden of shame that has me in cycles of hurt, especially in my relationships. Help me remember that I am not defined by my mistakes. Give me the strength to confess my sin and seek a godly sorrow that leads to true repentance. Holy Spirit, empower me to break free from this destructive cycle and experience your healing and grace. Restore my relationships and lead me in the freedom of your forgiveness. In Jesus' name, amen.

CONCLUSION

10

YOUR FUTURE SELF WILL THANK YOU

Justin and Trisha Davis

Justin

April 24, 2022, was the last Sunday of Hope City Church. We announced the closing of the church on April 10. The following Sunday was Easter, and we had 317 in attendance. Over 250 people attended our final service. While there was a loving and supportive group of about 80 people who journeyed with us through Covid and the trauma surrounding our dads not being our dads, a larger portion of our church didn't return to in-person services and that became too much to overcome. All I could think was, *If you guys had been here over the last year, we wouldn't be closing.*

Other than our separation in 2005, June 2021 to April 2022 was the most brutal year of my life. After the church closed, I felt like a failure. I was embarrassed. I spent weeks second-guessing my gifts, my ability to hear God's voice, my spiritual maturity, my leadership ability, and my calling as a pastor.

I failed as a leader. If I had been a better leader, I could have inspired people to buy into the vision more.

I failed as a pastor. If I were a better pastor, I would have grown the spiritual depth of our congregation more. I could have preached better messages. I could have equipped our leaders more.

I failed as a father. I asked my kids to leave all of their friends, their sports teams, their community, and their church and buy into my dream of this church. They gave their hearts and souls to Hope City only to have it close.

I was a failure as a husband. My wife believed in me. She trusted that I would figure it out, that I would find a way. We sold our house to keep the church open, and now we didn't have our house or the church.

I didn't just fail. I was a failure. I failed morally in 2005 with an affair. I failed in 2022 because I was so emotionally and spiritually exhausted, I couldn't be the leader the church needed.

We felt lost and shell-shocked. Two days after the last service of Hope City, I got a text message from a longtime friend, Jeff Henderson. Jeff is an incredible leader and pastor and had just transitioned off the staff of North Point Ministries in Atlanta. He told us how sorry he was to hear about the church closing. He was in town to speak at a conference and asked if we could do dinner the following evening. We went to P.F. Chang's and poured our hearts out over chicken lettuce wraps.

Jeff was just a few weeks away from releasing a new book called *What to Do Next*. He shared insights from his book and his own experience that were uplifting and encouraging to Trish and me. He then told us that we needed outside counsel and help determining our vocational and ministry next steps. We were too close to the situation to make our next move without getting outside perspective. He said we should consider a Life Plan.

We left dinner feeling like Jeff was providentially used by God to remind us that he sees us, cares for us, and still has a plan for us. There was so much wisdom in some of the things Jeff shared with us that a few days after our dinner, I reached out to an organization called The Patterson Center and inquired about participating in a Life Plan.

On June 14, 2022, Trish and I flew to Denver to spend three days on a Life Plan to try to determine what God wanted us to do with the rest of our lives. Our plans had failed, and we were willing to be obedient, but we wanted to be sure of our next step. I didn't want to fail again.

The next three days were painfully beautiful. We had to return to the very beginning of our relationship and identify the highs and lows of our marriage, ministry, and family. We were forced to confront our relationship patterns and how those contributed to the health or toxicity of our marriage and ministry.

One of the exercises our guide Michael had us complete is Our Life Vision. This is a seven-year vision for our life, family, and ministry. It took everything we learned about our wiring patterns, passions, gifts, experiences, fears, failures, successes, and desires to formulate a vision for our life seven years from now. One of the ways Michael quantified this exercise was making decisions that will cause "your future self to thank you."

Trisha

I'm sure you're ready for me to share how God showed up in the second half of Job's life. I remember Michael asking if I thought I was prepared for this. I was like, *Dude, we already paid for this; it's not like I can just leave and go skiing instead; I'm stuck here.* At least that's what I said in my head. What came out of my mouth was, "I just feel a bit fight club." Maybe I should've said the first thought. But he laughed, nonetheless. And then—ALL. THE. WORDS. Fell out of my mouth.

"Honestly, Michael, I'm a hard worker. I worked hard to love my staff and their families well through Covid. I worked hard to love my church family, even at the expense of mine. And if I hear one more podcaster talk about leading the church through Covid who didn't lead a church through Covid, I'm going to lose my mind! Because they have no idea how hard it was!"

You might think, *Oh boy, she's going full-on griping again*, which would've been an upgrade because I was feeling angry. I was so angry, but I'm not sure who I was angry with. I felt like Job in his season of affliction, and nobody had an answer or explanation as to why.

We had mentors, sages in the faith, and respected leaders in the church-planting world to whom we were accountable throughout the entire lifespan of the church. During the last six months of the church, all of those pastors were dealing with the collective trauma of leading their church through Covid and political and racially charged issues. They had their battles to fight, but I don't think any of them expected *ever* to hear the Davises say we were closing the church. They knew our character and our work ethic. They knew our redemption stories and were as perplexed as we were.

The last day with our life coach, I woke up super-anxious and mad as a raging bull that this was a mistake coming to this Life Plan. I told Justin, "I have less clarity about what the heck we are supposed to do with our lives than when we came." After two full days of life-planning exercises, on the third day, we walked into the meeting room to see all of them placed on ginormous sticky notes around the room.

Michael had placed almost thirty years of triumphs and failures on sticky notes in a timeline. He had us put a number 1 (living our best life) and 10 (living our worst nightmare) throughout our marriage. He then started connecting the numbers on our life timeline, and the results mirrored that of a rough rendering of the Rocky Mountains.

Michael asked me, "What do you see?"

I asked, "Do you want my real answer or the proper answer?"

He said, "Let's go with your honest answer."

"You know what I see when I look at the insanity of the extreme ups and downs of our almost thirty years together? I see a crap show!" Except I didn't use the word *crap*.

Michael was unfazed. "You know what I see? I see a life of resiliency." And with those words of truth being spoken over our Rocky Mountain life, I just started to sob.

How could one statement, one word, one new name for my pain be a turning point in my life? But it was a profound moment for me because Michael knew everything about us. And what he saw was the one choice we kept making as individuals, as a couple, as parents, and as leaders—resiliency.

My pain was given a new name.

Justin

Trisha and I have become more aware of the importance and impact of names over the last few years. When you discover your last name isn't what you thought it was for your entire life, there is an unknown attachment to your name. Names carry a legacy. Names carry reputation. Names carry heritage. Names carry identity.

In an article entitled "What's in a Name?" J. A. Taylor said, "The reason we spend so much time picking names for our children is that a name speaks to identity, and identity is a big deal."[1]

When we found out Trisha was pregnant with our oldest son, we had been married for four months and were students at Lincoln Christian College. In one of my Old Testament classes at Lincoln, I learned the Hebrew meaning of the name Micah, which is "one who seeks God." When we were told our baby would be a boy, I suggested to Trish we name him Micah, and we would pray he would live out the meaning of his name—one who seeks God. Although we weren't parents yet, we felt we had crushed assignment #1: baby's name.

Two years later, Trish surprised me on my birthday with the news that we were expecting baby number two. I use the term *surprised* because it's an understatement and *expecting* as the antithesis of what was true, because it came as a shock to me. After settling into this new reality, we knew we had to come up with an epic baby name. When you name your first kid "one who seeks God," you can't just name the second one Bob or Chuck (no offense to anyone named Bob or Chuck). It had to be biblical, purposeful, and prophetic. No pressure.

A few months into her second pregnancy, Trisha and I came up with the name Nathaniel. In the Old Testament, the name Nathaniel means "God has given," which would remind us that this child was a gift. *N* follows the letter *M* in the alphabet, so it made sense for Nathaniel to follow Micah. It seemed like a perfect fit until it wasn't—the day "Nathaniel" was born.

The delivery was very smooth until he was lifted out to have his cord cut. At that moment, the doctor could see that his umbilical cord was in a knot. Not knowing the severity of the situation, they took him over to the exam table and began to run tests on him more intensely than would typically happen. Thankfully, all the tests were normal, and he was healthy and beautiful.

There was only one problem. He didn't *look* like a Nathaniel. I told Trish, "I love the name Nathaniel, but he doesn't look like a Nathaniel."

She said, "We have pillows with the letter *N* embroidered on them. We have blankets with the name *Nathaniel* sewn on them. We have called him Nathaniel for the last six months."

I said, "Look at him, and see if you think he looks like a Nathaniel."

The nurse brought the baby to Trish, and Trish looked at him. "You're right; we can't name him Nathaniel. What are we going to name him?"

I asked the doctor when we had to decide on this name. He said they needed the name for the birth certificate, but we had some time. For the next six hours, we sat with our son in our arms, going through the Hebrew meaning of names in the Old Testament. Then we came to Elijah. Biblical? Check. Purposeful? It means "Jehovah is my God"—check. Prophetic? He was a prophet—check.

That evening, we introduced our family to Elijah Nathaniel Davis. If you know the story of Elijah in the Bible, he went out in a blaze of glory and was taken to heaven in a chariot of fire. Now, twenty-five years later, we can tell you that our son is way more of an Elijah than he is a Nathaniel. Names are a big deal.

Names Are a Big Deal to God

Proverbs 22:1 says, "A good name is more desirable than great riches; to be esteemed is better than silver or gold" (NIV). While that verse is more about reputation than the etymological meaning of a name, we believe names matter.

Names are a big deal to God too. Throughout the Scriptures, God was specific about the names of places and people. When God wanted to establish something new or create a new beginning, he would change a person's name. A name change signified a new calling or projected a person's future.

There are several examples of this in Scripture. Moses changed Hoshea's name to Joshua in Numbers 13:16. While it's only a slight change for us in English, the significance couldn't be greater in Hebrew. Hoshea means "salvation." Joshua means "Yahweh saves."

Every time Joshua's name was spoken, it was a reminder that it was Yahweh, not Hoshea, who saved the Israelites.

In Genesis 32:28, God changed Jacob's name to Israel. After Jacob spent much of his life scheming and deceiving to gain his brother's birthright and his father's blessing, God wrestled with Jacob and gave him a new name—Israel. Jacob, which means "deceiver," was given a new identity, Israel, "one who prevails with God."

In the New Testament, Jesus changed Simon's name to Peter, meaning "rock." Then Jesus followed up the name change with a vision for Peter's life and legacy: "And I tell you that you are Peter, and on this rock I will build my church, and the gates of Hades will not overcome it" (Matt. 16:18 NIV).

But the first name change happened in Genesis 17:5, when God changed Abram's name to Abraham. Abram means "exalted father," while Abraham means "father of many nations." Abraham's name was changed after God called Abraham to make one choice that would change everything: leave your father and mother and go to the land I will show you. Abram chose to be obedient, and God fulfilled his promise.

But look at what happened six chapters earlier in the book of Genesis.

> This is the account of Terah's family line.
>
> Terah became the father of Abram, Nahor and Haran. And Haran became the father of Lot. While his father Terah was still alive, Haran died in Ur of the Chaldeans, in the land of his birth. Abram and Nahor both married. The name of Abram's wife was

Sarai, and the name of Nahor's wife was Milkah; she was the daughter of Haran, the father of both Milkah and Iskah. Now Sarai was childless because she was not able to conceive.

Terah took his son Abram, his grandson Lot son of Haran, and his daughter-in-law Sarai, the wife of his son Abram, and together they set out from Ur of the Chaldeans to go to Canaan. But when they came to Harran, they settled there.

Terah lived 205 years, and he died in Harran. (Gen. 11:27–32 NIV)

Terah, which means "old fool" in Hebrew, was Abram's father. We don't know why, but "one day," Terah took his son Abram, his daughter-in-law Sarai, and his grandson Lot, and they moved away from Ur and headed to Canaan. Terah was going to what would eventually be the Promised Land. What if God came to Abram's father and offered to make him the father of many nations? What if God called Abram's dad to trust him in significant ways, to push past the unknown, and to demonstrate heroic faith? But he chose to stay comfortable. The only thing we know about Terah after they leave Ur is that "they stopped in Harran and settled there. Terah lived 205 years and died while still in Harran."

Could it be that those two words, "settled there," became the dysfunctional cycle of Abram's family? His dad had great intentions of going to Canaan, but he settled. He stopped short. He went part of the way but not all the way. He lived 205 years; the only thing we know about him is that he "died while still in

Harran." He never made it to where he could have been. He didn't reach his potential.

The very next passage in Genesis is chapter 12:1–3:

> The LORD had said to Abram, "Leave your native country, your relatives, and your father's family, and go to the land that I will show you. I will make you into a great nation. I will bless you and make you famous, and you will be a blessing to others. I will bless those who bless you and curse those who treat you with contempt. All the families on earth will be blessed through you."

What did Terah miss out on that he could have experienced if he had made one choice? As you are honest about your family history, what cycles need to be broken? As you identify unmet needs that have led to hurtful decisions, what is one choice you can make to leave them behind? As you inventory your relationships, what are the unhealthy cycles that keep them stuck or, even worse, toxic? You don't have to stay in Harran.

You Have What It Takes (Trisha)

People often ask me if I would endure all the pain again to become the person I am today and to have the marriage and family I now cherish. The answer is yes. But do I think you have to fail morally to have healthy relationships where you are fully known and fully loved? No.

I have learned throughout my life, in all the pain and beauty from ashes, that there is always a choice *you* can make. The hard part is that you can't choose for your spouse, parents, kids, friends, or faith community. Just like Abraham couldn't decide whether his dad would come with him, the one choice is always just for you.

You can absolutely inspire the people in your life to make the same choice, but even in their agreement, their journey will always differ from yours. While we may have shared experiences and faith, our experiences are as unique as our DNA. It's what makes *your* story so powerful. Your one choice may inspire someone else to make one choice. When the collection of those choices comes together, we get to witness the power of God moving in our lives. Sometimes, one choice or a lifetime of making one choice through the good and the bad shapes us into the people we are today.

We have the life we have today because, when our marriage fell apart, I chose to turn to God rather than run from him. Justin chose to pursue brokenness. "Brokenness, in God's eyes, is being so crushed by the sin and darkness of the world that we recognize there is no place to turn but to God."[2]

The one choice to trust God about the power of forgiveness, and Justin's one choice to pursue brokenness, have led to a million more healing choices. By creating a one-choice-at-a-time culture in our home, our kids have learned to make their own one choice to find healing from their hurts. Our one-choice culture has allowed relationships with family members to mend even if our pain isn't fully understood.

Breaking cycles in our lives begins with one choice. Today you are one choice away from change—one choice from breaking the cycles that hurt your relationships and hold you back.

One choice to obey.

One choice to trust.

One choice to forgive.

One choice to grieve.

One choice to do deep, painful work to break broken generational cycles.

Change happens one choice at a time, and YOU HAVE WHAT IT TAKES!

God's Commitment to Break Cycles

What is frustrating about trying to break cycles in our lives and relationships is that we feel like it is dependent on our ability or stamina. Have you ever gone on a diet or made a New Year's resolution to get in shape? You started off strong. You didn't eat carbs for a whole week. You went to the gym three times a week for a whole month. Then you looked in the mirror and didn't see any changes, so you gave up.

When you choose to break the cycles we've identified in this book, there will be resistance. It will not be easy. You will start to think you can't do it. You aren't good enough. You don't have what it takes. The truth is that none of us have the ability to overcome sin on our own. None of us have the strength to defeat shame on our own. None of us have the resilience to forgive those who have wounded us on our own.

Our capacity to break cycles in our lives is directly proportional to our willingness to understand our past, acknowledge our hurts, confess our sins, and completely surrender them to the redeeming power of Christ. God promises to re-create you—that is how committed he is to breaking cycles in your life. God doesn't want you to be better; he wants you to be brand-new.

> And I will give you a new heart, and I will put a new spirit in you. I will take out your stony, stubborn heart and give you a tender, responsive heart. (Ezek. 36:26)

> And the one sitting on the throne said, "Look, I am making everything new!" (Rev. 21:5)

> Put on your new nature, and be renewed as you learn to know your Creator and become like him. In this new life, it doesn't matter if you are a Jew or a Gentile, circumcised or uncircumcised, barbaric, uncivilized, slave, or free. Christ is all that matters, and he lives in all of us. (Col. 3:10–11)

Your New Name

God has a hope and a future for you, and he hasn't brought you this far to leave you here. He plans to use everything you've gone through to restore and redeem his purpose for your life. God is still changing names. You have a new life, a new heart, a new future. In Christ, you are transformed:

> Wounded to healed
> Broken to restored
> Captive to free
> Lost to found
> Stranger to friend
> Insecure to secure
> Guilty to forgiven

You Are New

> Therefore, if anyone is in Christ, the new creation has come: The old has gone, the new is here! (2 Cor. 5:17 NIV)

You are not your past. You are not your failures. You are not your parents. You are not your sister. You are not your regrets. You are not your sin. You are not your divorce. You are not your weight. You are not your unemployment. You are not the choices someone else made for you. You are not your brokenness. You are not your bitterness. You are not your abuse. You are not your loneliness. You are not your marital status. You are not your tax bracket. You are not your crisis.

You are loved. You are forgiven. You are redeemed. You are called. You are chosen. You are set apart. You are valued. You are gifted. You are prized. You are reconciled. You are noticed. You are pursued. You are a child of the King. You are a co-heir with Christ.

You are a royal priesthood. You are adored, cherished, and treasured by the God of this universe. That is who you are.

You Are Complete

Don't let anyone capture you with empty philosophies and high-sounding nonsense that come from human thinking and from the spiritual powers of this world, rather than from Christ. For in Christ lives all the fullness of God in a human body. (Col. 2:8–9)

Every day, people and messages will try to capture you with the empty philosophy that you are not complete. You aren't complete until your marriage is healed. You aren't complete until you are married. You aren't complete until you have a new job. You aren't complete until you become a parent. You aren't complete until you have a bigger house, a nicer office, and a different tax bracket. You aren't complete until you finally break the cycle that's followed you for years.

In Christ, you are complete. You don't have to marry anyone, fix anything, achieve anything, or prove anything to one day become complete. Your identity with God is secure through the person of Jesus Christ.

You Are God's Masterpiece

For we are God's masterpiece. He has created us anew in Christ Jesus, so we can do the good things he planned for us long ago. (Eph. 2:10)

For centuries, a painting called *Christ Mocked*, by the Florentine artist Cimabue, was believed to be missing. The painting depicted Jesus' crucifixion. But in 2019, it turned up in the kitchen of a ninety-year-old woman living in the French countryside.

The painting hung above a hot plate in the kitchen until an auctioneer came to the woman's house to prepare for her move. According to CNN,[3] the painting was worth $6.5 million, but actually sold at auction for $26.8 million—four times the expected price.[4]

The masterpiece was worth so much more than the kitchen in which it hung. Value isn't determined by what someone thinks something to be worth. Value isn't determined by an appraisal of something. Value is always determined by what someone is willing to pay. The woman thought the painting was worth only kitchen decor. The appraiser valued this masterpiece at $6.5 million. But someone saw it as so much more valuable. They paid four times its projected value.

God sees you as his masterpiece no matter what you think about yourself. You are so valuable to God that he paid the price of his Son's life to restore your identity and determine your worth.

A Note from Your Future Self

As we sat in a room in Denver, Colorado, in July 2022, with the history of our entire life together spread out on huge Post-it notes, there was nothing we could do about the church closing. We couldn't take away the affair, our financial mistakes, or our dads not being our biological fathers. Those choices were gone and out of our control.

But we could look at our life, marriage, and family seven years into the future. Who do we want to be? What type of relationship do we want with our kids? What core values do we desire for our family to embody? What choices will we make so our future selves will thank us?

You can't go back and change your parents or their decisions. You can't undo the abuse or abandonment you may have experienced when you were younger. You can't take away the arguments you've had or the harsh words you've spoken to those you love most. You can't change the dynamics of your first marriage or make up for the mistakes you made that dissolved a relationship. The choices you made ten years ago—relationally, financially, vocationally, and maritally—have accumulated into the life you have today.

But what if your future self could write you a thank-you note for your choice today to break the cycles in your life, marriage, and family? How powerful would it be to get a letter from you from seven years in the future, describing your healthy marriage because you broke hurtful patterns in your dating life today? How freeing would it be to have your future self describe your financial situation five years from now because you chose to stop retail therapy and get a handle on your finances? How burden-lifting would it be to get a thank-you note from your future self, describing the freedom you have from sexual brokenness because you chose to be honest about it today? How satisfying would it be to get a letter from your future self, recounting your life-giving relationship with your future adult kids because you chose to break family cycles today? How encouraging would it be to get a note from the future version of you, sharing how close of a friendship you have with your spouse because you chose to be vulnerable and transparent with your husband or wife today?

Here is what is so powerful about where you are today. You can choose what type of note your future self will write you based on the choices you make today.

That is your choice today. Who do you want to be five years from now, seven years from now? What choice will you make to take a step in that direction? What cycle needs to be broken? What do you need to surrender?

One choice changes everything.

ACKNOWLEDGMENTS

Justin and Trisha

To our "Bigs" and daughters-in-love, Micah, Rylei, Elijah, Emma, and Isaiah, no words could express the depth of our gratitude for each of you. Your love during this incredible, hard season has forever marked us. Thank you for your presence, kindness, wisdom, laughter, and prayers. You are all priceless treasures. We love you!

To our "Littles": Jailyn—we hope this book empowers you to be a cycle breaker and write an incredible story with your life. Janiyah—thank you for teaching us how to be girl parents. Your wisdom and love for people teach us something new every day! Keep shining your light!

To our Hope City Church family: We will forever cherish the incredible and wild ride we had together. Although our time was cut short, we know God continues to use each of you to remind a broken world that HOPE CHANGES EVERYTHING. We love you and continue to cheer wildly for you!

Jill Vosberg: Thank you for relentlessly pursuing truth and grace in managing all things RefineUs. Your dedication and hard work made writing this book possible, and we're deeply grateful to have you on our team!

Dan Balow and the Steve Laube Agency: Thank you, Dan, for your kindness, patience, and advocacy as we poured our heart out to you before we poured it into the book. Thank you for representing our message so well.

Michael Covington and our David C Cook team: Thank you for your belief in us and the message of this book. Thank you for your patience and care every step of the way. We are grateful to partner with you to share this message.

Jeff Henderson: Sitting at a table in P.F. Chang's, you became our real-life version of Rocky's trainer, Mickey Goldmill. You gave us our first *one choice*, "Don't give up." Thank you for being FOR the Davises. We are excited to celebrate with all the movie popcorn!

Derwin and Vicki Gray: Thank you for your friendship, your belief in our message, and your love of our family. God has used you both to breathe encouragement into our souls!

Michael Chiarelli: Thank you for providing a safe place to come, broken in mind, body, and spirit, yet showing us how resilient faith in God, ourselves, and each other has been and continues to move mountains.

Trisha

Mom and Dad: This book is our redemption story. I have cherished being your daughter, and I love you both so very much!

To my brother Frankie Lopez, thank you for always showing up with your unshakable love, belief, and belonging through all these broken and beautiful years. I love you!

Meredith Boaz, Kylie Arceo, and Glory Adepetu, thank you for being an inspiring example of grit and grace. Your unwavering commitment to growth and encouragement has paved the way for me to become the best version of myself. I'm forever grateful for you!

To my sis Julie Lopez, nieces Ky, Jocey, Miya, Madi, Emmerson, nephews Evan and Jordan, Pops, Momma Lisa, and Ruben: I love you, and I love being a part of your tribe!

To my counselor, Stephanie Castle: Thank you for providing a safe place to process, grieve, and hope again. This book would not exist without you.

Angi Goodwin, Brooker Castaneda, and Jodi Knox-Holub, thank you for thirty years of unwavering love, laughter, and friendship. I can't imagine this life without you!

Lori Langebartles, thank you for sushi, laughter, and friendship through so many seasons of life. I love doing life with you!

To Oriana and Suzy and my incredible Zumba community: Gracias, 谢谢, धन्यवाद, شکراً, Ευχαριστώ, תודה, Na gode, Merci, Obrigada, Grazie, THANK YOU for making our class an incredible global community and giving *belonging* a whole new meaning. I treasure each of you!

To the love of my life and best friend, Justin. Your resilient love for God, me, and our kids has given me a glimpse of heaven on earth. Thank you for choosing God, choosing us, and choosing never to give up. My love for you goes beyond what words could express. You have my heart forever and always.

Justin

To my family: Mom and Phillip, Meredith, Jacob, and Jonah, thank you for your willingness to go through the deep waters with me. Our family isn't perfect, but I hope you can see how God redeems more of our story each day.

Scott and Lou Wentz, thank you for your consistent belief in me, our ministry, and the message of hope and redemption. Thank you for your investment in our family over the years. We love you!

Chris and Cindy Johnson, thank you for showing up and being a shoulder to cry on and a hand to high-five. You are friends we love like family.

Toni Timberman, thank you for responding to a random message on Ancestry.com. You helped connect dots and bring closure in a way I didn't know I needed.

RefineUs Community: Thank you to so many who have invited us into their churches, email inboxes, and bookshelves through our conferences, newsletters, and books. We pray our story inspires you to make one choice that brings change.

Trisha, thank you for saving my life and loving me like Jesus. I admire you and adore you. Your choice to pursue healing changed our family's trajectory and our story's ending. You have my heart.

NOTES

Chapter One

1. Terry Gaspard, "Timing Is Everything When It Comes to Marriage Counseling," The Gottman Institute, accessed August 15, 2024, www.gottman.com/blog/timing-is-everything-when-it-comes-to-marriage-counseling.

2. Sarah Pruitt, "Here Are 6 Things Albert Einstein Never Said," History Channel, accessed August 15, 2024, www.history.com/news/here-are-6-things-albert-einstein-never-said.

3. Henry Cloud, *Necessary Endings: The Employees, Business, and Relationships That All of Us Have to Give Up in Order to Move Forward* (New York: HarperCollins, 2010), 7, Kindle.

4. Peter Scazzero, *Emotionally Healthy Spirituality: It's Impossible to Be Spiritually Mature, While Remaining Emotionally Immature* (Grand Rapids, MI: Zondervan, 2017), 98.

5. Brené Brown, *I Thought It Was Just Me (but It Isn't): Making the Journey from "What Will People Think?" to "I Am Enough"* (New York: Avery, 2007), 75.

6. Brad Brenner, "5 Unmet Needs That May Cause Psychological Issues in Adulthood," Therapy Group of NYC, accessed August 15, 2024, https://nyctherapy.com/therapists-nyc-blog/5-unmet-needs-that-may-cause-psychological-issues-in-adulthood/.

7. Kim Samuel, "The New Psychology of Belonging," *Psychology Today*, accessed August 15, 2024, www.psychologytoday.com/intl/blog/the-power-of-belonging/202304/the-new-psychology-of-belonging.

Chapter Two

1. Wikipedia, "Tribe of Ephraim," accessed August 15, 2024, https://en.wikipedia.org/wiki/Tribe_of_Ephraim.

2. H. Norman Wright, *When the Past Won't Let You Go: Find the Healing That Helps You Move On* (Eugene, OR: Harvest House, 2016), 10.

3. Elyssa Barbash, "Different Types of Trauma: Small 't' versus Large 'T,'" *Psychology Today*, accessed August 15, 2024, www.psychologytoday.com/us/blog/trauma-and-hope/201703/different-types-trauma-small-t-versus-large-t.

Chapter Three

1. Susan David, *Emotional Agility: Get Unstuck, Embrace Change, and Thrive in Work and Life* (New York: Avery, 2016), 165.

2. David, *Emotional Agility*, 165.

3. "Understanding Grief and Loss: An Overview," HealGrief, accessed August 15, 2024, https://healgrief.org/understanding-grief/.

4. Ruth Davis Konigsberg, *The Truth about Grief: The Myth of Its Five Stages and the New Science of Loss* (New York: Simon & Schuster, 2011), n.p.

5. Patrick Tyrrell, et al., "Kubler-Ross Stages of Dying and Subsequent Models of Grief," National Library of Medicine, accessed August 15, 2024, www.ncbi.nlm.nih.gov/books/NBK507885.

6. "12 Phases of Grief Aren't Linear and That's Okay," Heart in Diamond, accessed August 15, 2024, www.heart-in-diamond.com/cremation-diamonds/grief-stages.html.

7. "12 Phases," www.heart-in-diamond.com/cremation-diamonds/grief-stages.html.

Chapter Four

1. Curt Singh, "The Children's Museum of Indianapolis Is the World's Largest Children's Museum," Life in Indy, accessed August 15, 2024, https://lifeinindy.com/things-to-do/the-childrens-museum-of-indianapolis/.

2. Craig Bloem, "Why Successful People Wear the Same Thing Every Day," *Inc.*, accessed August 15, 2024, www.inc.com/craig-bloem/this-1-unusual-habit-helped-make-mark-zuckerberg-steve-jobs-dr-dre-successful.html.

3. Sara Berg, MS, "What Doctors Wish Patients Knew about Decision Fatigue," AMA, November 19, 2021, www.ama-assn.org/delivering-care/public-health/what-doctors-wish-patients-knew-about-decision-fatigue.

4. William Worley, "Why Steve Jobs Always Wore the Same Thing," accessed August 15, 2024, www.cnn.com/2015/10/09/world/gallery/decision-fatigue-same-clothes/index.html.

5. Worley, "Why Steve Jobs."

6. Worley, "Why Steve Jobs."

7. Mariel Buqué, *Break the Cycle: A Guide to Healing Intergenerational Trauma* (New York: Dutton, 2024), 13–14.

Chapter Five

1. Dictionary.com, s.v. "blame," accessed August 15, 2014, www.dictionary.com/browse/blame.

2. Ana Gonzales, "Why We Blame Others," Citron Hennessey, accessed August 15, 2024, www.privatetherapy.com/blog/blame-and-responsibility/.

3. Mike McClure Jr., "I Quit Blaming Others," YouTube, accessed August 15, 2024, www.youtube.com/live/4F60-9qAXv4.

4. Ilona Jerabek and Deborah Muoio, "It Wasn't My Fault: New Study Looks at Why People Hate Admitting Mistakes," ResearchGate, accessed August 15, 2024, www.researchgate.net/publication/335312787_It_Wasn't_My_Fault_New_Study _Looks_At_Why_People_Hate_Admitting_Mistakes.

5. Alison Cook, *I Shouldn't Feel This Way: Name What's Hard, Tame Your Guilt, and Transform Self-Sabotage into Brave Action* (Nashville: Nelson, 2024), 160.

6. Dictionary.com, s.v. "victimization," accessed August 15, 2024, www.dictionary. com/browse/victimization.

7. Brennan Manning, *Abba's Child: The Cry of the Heart for Intimate Belonging* (Colorado Springs: NavPress, 2015), 82, Kindle.

8. Mariel Buqué, *Break the Cycle: A Guide to Healing Intergenerational Trauma* (New York: Dutton, 2024), 70–71.

9. McClure, "I Quit Blaming Others."

Chapter Six

1. Dictionary.com, s.v. "resentment," accessed August 15, 2024, www.dictionary. com/browse/resentment.

2. *Inside Out 2*, directed by Kelsey Mann (Emeryville, CA: Pixar Animation Studios, 2024).

3. *Inside Out 2*.

4. CNN, accessed August 15, 2024, www.cnn.com/TRANSCRIPTS/1508/31/ cnr.08.html.

5. "Forgiveness: Your Health Depends on It," Johns Hopkins Medicine, accessed August 15, 2024, www.hopkinsmedicine.org/health/wellness-and-prevention /forgiveness-your-health-depends-on-it.

6. Charles L. Quarles, "Matthew," in *CSB Study Bible*, ed. Edwin A. Blum and Trevin Wax (Nashville: Holman Bible Publishers, 2017), 1533.

7. Quarles, "Matthew," in *CSB Study Bible*.

8. Latasha Morrison, *Be the Bridge: Pursuing God's Heart for Racial Reconciliation* (Colorado Springs: WaterBrook, 2019), 117.

Chapter Seven

1. E. Ray Clendenen, "Fear," ed. Chad Brand et al., *Holman Illustrated Bible Dictionary* (Nashville: Holman Bible Publishers, 2003), 562.

2. Robert Maurer and Michelle Gifford, *Mastering Fear: Harness Emotion to Achieve Excellence in Work, Health, and Relationships* (Wayne, NJ: Career Press, 2016), 23.

3. Dictionary.com, s.v. "amygdala," accessed September 20, 2024, www.dictionary.com/browse/amygdala.

4. Lindsay Wilson, "The Book of Job and the Fear of God," *Tyndale Bulletin*, accessed August 15, 2024, https://Doi.Org/10.53751/001c.30397.

5. Wilson, "Book of Job."

6. Maurer and Gifford, *Mastering Fear*, 23.

7. Maurer and Gifford, *Mastering Fear*, 36.

8. Maurer and Gifford, *Mastering Fear*, 39.

9. Maurer and Gifford, *Mastering Fear*, 41.

Chapter Eight

1. Andy Stanley, accessed August 15, 2024, https://twitter.com/andystanley/status/19767709604.

2. Natalie Baker, "We're Only as Sick as Our Secrets," American Addiction Centers, accessed August 15, 2024, https://recovery.org/were-only-as-sick-as-our-secrets/.

3. Shawn Johnson, *Attacking Anxiety: From Panicked and Depressed to Alive and Free* (Nashville: Thomas Nelson, 2022), 120, Kindle.

4. Steve Carter, *The Thing Beneath the Thing: What's Hidden Inside (and What God Helps Us Do about It)* (Nashville: Thomas Nelson, 2021), 47.

5. Johnson, *Attacking Anxiety*, 121.

6. Brennan Manning, *Abba's Child: The Cry of the Heart for Intimate Belonging* (Colorado Springs: NavPress, 2015), 159, Kindle.

Chapter Nine

1. Brené Brown, "Listening to Shame," TED, accessed August 15, 2024, www.ted.com/talks/brene_brown_listening_to_shame?language=en&subtitle=en&delay=1m.

2. Lewis Smedes, *Shame and Grace: Healing the Shame We Don't Deserve* (New York: HarperCollins, 1993), 11.

3. Merriam-Webster's Online Dictionary, s.v. "guilt," accessed November 18, 2024, www.merriam-webster.com/dictionary/guilt.

4. Passion City Church, "Chain Breaker—The Chain of Shame," YouTube, accessed August 15, 2024, www.youtube.com/watch?v=klLQWelSjUM.

5. Merriam-Webster's Online Dictionary, s.v. "shame," accessed August 15, 2024, www.merriam-webster.com/dictionary/shame.

6. Brené Brown, *Daring Greatly: How the Courage to Be Vulnerable Transforms the Way We Live, Love, Parent, and Lead* (New York: Gotham Books, 2012), 71.

7. Brown, *Daring Greatly*, 69.

8. Smedes, *Shame and Grace*, 6–7.

9. Brown, *Daring Greatly*, 72–73.

10. Smedes, *Shame and Grace*, 83.

11. Holly Meyer, "What New Lifeway Research Survey Says about Why Young Adults Are Dropping Out of Church," *Tennessean*, accessed August 15, 2024, www.tennessean.com/story/news/religion/2019/01/15/lifeway-research-survey-says-young-adults-dropping-out-church/2550997002/.

12. Passion City Church, "Chain Breaker."

13. Brown, *Daring Greatly*, 109.

14. Alison Cook, *I Shouldn't Feel This Way: Name What's Hard, Tame Your Guilt, and Transform Self-Sabotage into Brave Action* (Nashville: Thomas Nelson, 2024), 7.

15. Jeremy Sutton, "Shame Resilience Theory: Advice from Brené Brown," PositivePsychology.com, accessed August 15, 2024, https://positivepsychology.com/shame-resilience-theory/.

16. Brown, "Listening to Shame."

Chapter Ten

1. J. A. Taylor, "What's in a Name?," Medium, accessed August 15, 2024, https://medium.com/koinonia/whats-in-a-name-9fee77f53a54.

2. "What Is Brokenness?," Cord of 3, accessed September 20, 2024, www.cordofthreecounseling.org/2019/10/02/what-is-brokenness/.

3. Susie Heller, "A Long-Lost Painting Believed to Be Worth $6.5 Million Was Found in a Random Woman's Kitchen in France," *Business Insider*, accessed August 15, 2024, www.insider.com/lost-christ-mocked-painting-found-in-home-french-woman-2019-9.

4. Lia Ryerson and Frank Olito, "A Woman Learned That a Painting She Had Hanging in Her Kitchen for Years Was Worth $26.8 Million," *Business Insider*, accessed August 15, 2024, www.insider.com/what-is-my-stuff-worth-2018-3#a-woman-learned-that-a-painting-she-had-hanging-in-her-kitchen-for-years-was-worth-268-million-2.

DAVID C COOK

JOIN US.
SPREAD THE GOSPEL.
CHANGE THE WORLD.

We believe in equipping the local church with Christ-centered resources that empower believers, even in the most challenging places on earth.

We trust that God is *always* at work, in the power of Jesus and the presence of the Holy Spirit, inviting people into relationship with Him.

We are committed to spreading the gospel throughout the world—across villages, cities, and nations. We trust that the Word of God will transform lives and communities by bringing light to the darkness.

As a global ministry with a 150-year legacy, David C Cook is dedicated to this mission. Each time you purchase a resource or donate, you're supporting a ministry—helping spread the gospel, disciple believers, and raise up leaders in some of the world's most underserved regions.

Your support fuels this mission.
Your partnership sends the gospel where it's needed most.

Discover more. Be the difference.
Visit DavidCCook.org/Donate